CUSTER

CUSTER

Man & Myth

MICHAEL ANGLO

JUPITER · LONDON

First published in 1976 by
JUPITER BOOKS(LONDON) LIMITED
167 Hermitage Road, London N4

SBN 904041 49 2

Composed on the Monotype in 11/14pt Baskerville 169
by HBM Typesetting Limited, Chorley, Lancashire

Printed and bound by R. J. Acford Limited,
Chichester, Sussex.

Contents

VOICE FROM THE PLAINS

"All same old story. White men come, build chu-chu [railroad] through reservation. White men yawpy-yawpy [talk]. Say: 'Good Indian, good Indian; we want land. We give muz-es-kow [money]; liliota muz-es-kow [plenty money].' Indian say, 'Yes.' What Indian get? Wah-nee-che [nothing]. Some day white man want move Indian. White men yawpy-yawpy: 'Good Indian, good Indian; give good Indian liliota muz-es-kow.' What Indian get? Wah-nee-che. Some day white man want half big reservation. He come Indian. Yawpy-yawpy: 'Good Indian; we give Indian liliota muz-es-kow.' Indian heap fool. He say, 'Yes.' What Indian get? Wah-nee-che. All same old story. 'Good Indian, good Indian.' Get nothing."

HARPER'S MAGAZINE, C. 1892.

THE CASE OF CUSTER

SINCE THAT DAY HE DIED IN BATTLE ON THE LITTLE BIG HORN, MANY CONTROVERSIAL books have been written on General Armstrong Custer, and newspapers and magazines over the years have featured articles on him, the more recent tending to harp on his faults and supposed faults with considerable bias.

Original source material is wide but, of course, limited and it is doubtful now that any new material or historical documents on the subject will be brought to light. All writers and students can do is examine original source material, the various assessments and speculations and make their own assessments, speculations and conclusions according to the way they see it, to become Custerphobes or Custerphiles. Or they may be moved by the quirks of their own natures to choose sides in much the same way as people often do inexplicably, to become reactionaries or radicals, Republicans or Democrats, Spurs or Arsenal supporters.

It is widely believed persons serving on a jury decide a case on evidence, hard evidence; not hearsay or personal opinions. In the case of Custer the options still seem to be wide open.

But I must tell this tale thus for the nonce
When men cry mum and keep such silence long,
Then stones must speak, else dead men shall have wrong.

George Gascoigne (16th cent).

ACKNOWLEDGEMENTS

I AM GRATEFUL TO CUSTER EXPERT DANIEL POSNER, ANTIQUARIAN BOOKSELLER OF Charing Cross, for advice and material for writing this book. No lover of generals, it was partly due to Daniel Posner that I first began to see General Custer in a sympathetic light and accept the idea that it is possible to be a general without being a donkey.

I gratefully acknowledge and thank all those researchers and gatherers of source material whose works have made so much information on Custer so easily accessible.

Since the naked body of George Armstrong Custer was found with the mutilated remains of his men on the battlefield of the Little Big Horn, millions of words have been written about Custer's Last Stand. All sorts of claims have been made at one time or another, but so far it seems nobody has ever claimed to have got the story straight from the horse's mouth. This is very surprising, to be sure, for the sole survivor of the Seventh Cavalry, on the field of the Last Stand about which controversy has long since raged, was Comanche, a sleek gelding, badly wounded in the battle. It had belonged to Captain Myles Keogh, one of Custer's troop commanders who died with him. The horse was nursed back to health, but was never ridden again. It died aged twenty-eight, fifteen years after the battle, in all that time, it is believed, without ever murmuring a word.

Had it been possible for the white invaders of North America to enslave completely the indigenous population as a labour force, the Indians might have been as numerous and as integrated as the Negroes in America are today. But the Indians could not bend with the wind of change and were broken. They were harassed, cheated, persecuted, murdered and all but exterminated. The survivors were herded like cattle into reservations and there left, neglected, for years.

The Indians had battled hopelessly and ever more savagely for survival as the flood of voracious Europeans inundated more and more of their lands, but there was never, nor could there have ever been, a complete coalition of Indian forces to make a stand against the whites until Sitting Bull assembled in Dakota in 1876 the mightiest force of Indian warriors the white men had ever to contend with. It was then far too late for the Indian, after three hundred years of white encroachment, to halt, let alone reverse, the tidal wave sweeping across the Western frontier, but with the Civil War resolved and a united country making ready to celebrate the hundredth anniversary of the American Declaration of Independence on July 4, 1876, the United States was shocked to learn that at the Battle of the Little Big Horn a mighty force of Indians, composed mainly of Sioux and Cheyennes, had won a signal victory over the vaunted U.S. Cavalry and that General Custer, a national hero thought to have been invincible, had died with his men.

The Seventh Cavalry

GEORGE ARMSTRONG CUSTER WAS BORN AT NEW RUMLEY, OHIO, ON DECEMBER 5, 1839. His father was a blacksmith and it is possible that it was in the heat-laden atmosphere of the forge, watching muscular, sweating horses snorting, whinnying, restless, with the clangour of the hammer on the anvil amid showers of sparks, that young Custer was first charged with the martial excitement of horses.

However, at the age of ten, Custer was taken to live with Mrs. David Reed, his half sister, at Monroe, a small town on the Raisin River, Michigan. The family was not considered to be socially acceptable by the more prominent Monroe citizens who included Judge Daniel S. Bacon, Custer's future father-in-law, but social and economic handicaps did not daunt young Custer. By the time he was seventeen he was teaching in a small country school and at the age of eighteen he was admitted to the Military Academy at West Point.

At the Academy, Custer was more noted among his tutors and fellow students for his exuberance and apparent lack of responsibility than for his mastery of military manuals. He was not inclined to go by the book, probably realising early that the book is no substitute for military instinct, field experience and initiative. He was fond of playing practical jokes, often dangerous. He was charged and punished on numerous occasions for various military misdemeaners arising from carelessness in his uniform and general military appearance, and his independence of attitude and approach to outmoded barrack room and parade ground discipline.

Yet despite all this, which in the case of another cadet would have probably meant dismissal from the Academy, the very faults Custer displayed must have marked him as the type of cadet who makes a good soldier in the field. Even when, immediately after graduation, while acting officer of the guard at camp, he failed to interfere in a fight between two cadets, Custer was merely reprimanded.

Custer graduated in June 1861, four years after entering the Military Academy, at the bottom of his class, but there is no doubt that the result hardly reflected his ability. It is undeniable that he was able to assimilate knowledge and acquire skills in subjects that interested him and he was interested in literature, history and dramatics. He wrote well and later contributed regularly to *The Galaxy*, a literary fortnightly magazine. The articles were later published as a book under the title of *Wild Life on the Plains*. His style is breezy, descriptive, and spiced here and there with quotations from Shakespeare.

With the outbreak of the American Civil War in April 1861, Custer went immediately to Washington and was entrusted by General Scott with despatches for General McDowell, and was assigned for duty as a second-lieutenant in the Fifth Cavalry. He was on hand to take part in the first general battle of the war, at Bull Run. He fought at Antietam, the Shenandoah Campaign and Appomattox. In 1862 he was a captain and by 1863 he had risen to the rank of Brigadier-General of Volunteers by dint of his brilliant success as a cavalry leader. At the age of twenty-three, Custer, known as the "boy general," was given command of the Michigan Brigade, and the newspapers of the north revelled in his exploits.

Custer was certainly aware of the value of publicity and the benefits to be derived from a colourful appearance. He designed eye-catching uniforms for himself which distinguished him from his fellow officers. These, and his dashing exploits in the field, attracted the attention of news correspondents in the same way as did Montgomery, Patton and Rommel in World War II. He was a ruthless fighting soldier and his fearless forays and brilliantly fought actions were glorified in the press from the *New York Times* to *The Times* of London. His men were proud to bask in the glory he reflected.

At Monroe in 1864, when he was twenty-five, Custer married Elizabeth Bacon, the girl of his dreams. The Bacons and the Reeds had always moved in different social circles in class-conscious Monroe, but Judge Bacon, the father of Libbie Bacon, no doubt impressed by the meteoric rise of the hitherto socially unacceptable young Custer, suppressed his objections and, despite some reservations about Custer's future status, agreed to the marriage. The judge was happy to preen himself in the glow of Custer's exploits which the press were giving extensive coverage. A month after his marriage to Libbie, the cover of *Harper's Weekly* depicted Custer leading a raid on the supply depot at Charlottesville, deep in Confederate territory.

During Sheridan's Shenandoah Campaign it was Custer who led the way with his victorious charge at Cedar Creek, and when Sheridan blocked the last retreat of Robert E. Lee, Custer's raids south toward the Appomattox, smashing the Confederate cavalry and harrassing Lee's infantry, opened the way to Union victory.

Custer was excited by the idea of close combat and never shied away from leading a wild cavalry charge, thrilling to the thunder of hooves, flapping guidons and yelling cavalrymen in the smoke and dust of battle. It was generally agreed by those who saw him in action that he never showed outward signs of fear. Caught up in the fever of confused fighting, he seemed oblivious to the thought of death or injury, plunging into the thick of battle without hesitation, expecting his men to feel as he did and do likewise. As an officer he took

13

calculated risks which, because of their sheer audacity and boldness in execution, were usually successful. Custer believed in seizing the initiative whenever he saw a possibility of forcing a victory, even when it was necessary to re-assess orders, never baulking when it came to pushing his men as hard as he was prepared to push himself. He was impatient and intolerant of those of his officers who were inclined to carp or who seemed slow on the uptake, and at times he could be insensitive to the feelings of his men, as if unable to understand why their enthusiasm did not match his own. When campaigning it seemed he regarded his men and horses as appurtenances of war, and battle their primary function.

Most of the recruits had joined the Seventh Cavalry Regiment after the Civil War, specifically for service against the Indians of the Great Plains and were drawn from the ranks of ex-soldiers and unemployed, immigrants and refugees from Europe, who had failed to find a place in the new country, and most of whom could not speak English nor understand orders. There were also criminals on the run and "drop-outs", and many regiments of the U.S. Army were akin to units of the French Foreign Legion except that the training was poor and they lacked the discipline that welded the Legion into a formidable fighting force.

With the end of the Civil War, the Army had returned to its peacetime role. Custer spent the next six months on occupation duties in Texas and when his commission as major-general of volunteers expired in January 1866, he had to revert to his former rank as captain in the regular army. With the demobilisation of the bulk of the armies, opportunities for promotion would be small and Custer, uncertain about his future prospects, was considering a new peacetime career. But in July the reorganisation of the military establishment of the United States provided Custer with a chance for which he had been hoping. Four new cavalry regiments were formed, the Seventh and Eighth composed of white troops; the Ninth and the Tenth of Negroes. The officers were being chosen solely on merit and qualifications from veterans of the Union Army.

Custer was commissioned lieutenant-colonel, with a brevet rank of major-general in the regular army, appointed second-in-command of the Seventh Cavalry and posted to Fort Riley, Kansas. In actual fact, Custer served as the effective commander of the unit for the rest of his life, as the regiment's colonel, and in common with many regimental colonels during the period, was usually away on staff duties for most of the time. But the situation for the officers at Fort Riley was not a happy one. Many of them with fine war records had been demoted from the ranks they had held in the Civil War and were resentful of having to serve in subordinate capacities. Many of them were older than their new commanding officer and their envy and jealousy, without a doubt, helped sow the seeds of dissension and discord that seemed to bedevil the smooth working of the regiment right from the start. Moreover Custer, still a young man with wide interests and very much in love with his wife, did not have to rely on the company of his fellow officers outside of duty, which is not to say that he remained entirely aloof from regimental recreational activities.

Custer and Libbie, the woman he loved and who loved him. They risked everything to be together.

The senior major of the regiment, Major Alfred Gibbs, had been a brevet major-general during the war, and the second major, Wickliffe Cooper, had been the colonel of a Kentucky Cavalry regiment. Frederick Benteen who had been a lieutenant-colonel was just a captain commanding a troop of cavalry. Other officers who joined the regiment before the end of the year included Captain Myles Keogh, an Irishman who had served in the Papal Guards, Lieutenant W. W. Cook, and Lieutenant Thomas Custer, brother of George Armstrong, a first-class fighting man who had won two Congressional Medals of Honour in the Civil War.

Custer spent the winter of 1866–7 supervising the drilling and training of his men for a campaign against the Indians in the spring. The task of welding the homogenous elements of his command into an efficient fighting force for such a purpose was an unenviable one. Custer, although a seasoned soldier, had had

15

no experience of Indian fighting. The training consisted mainly of repetitious routine drilling, monotonous and soul destroying for the most part, and useless in the field. It seems unusual that a man of Custer's rebellious nature should have concentrated on this means to maintain the discipline and efficiency of his troops, but the drills did help to improve the quality of their horsemanship and their precision of manoeuvre became a regular feature on the parade ground.

Like most frontier forts and posts of the period, Fort Riley was isolated, with few facilities for the amusement of troops off duty. The food varied from very bad to indifferent. Barrack rooms were miserable, badly lighted, badly heated and badly ventilated. The men were rarely required to bath and in any case facilities were limited. Outpost duties around the fort were boring and tedious. But such conditions are usual in the field in any war and in any army. Of course, the officers fared considerably better. This also is usual in nearly every army and few officers had any rapport with their men. Custer gave scant consideration to the creature comforts of his men during the training period, preparing them for the hardships they were bound to experience in the active campaigning ahead.

The Spring Campaign of 1867, instigated and led by Major General Hancock, commanding the Department of the Missouri, was against hostile elements of Sioux, Cheyenne and Arapaho. Ostensibly the expedition was to intimidate the hostiles, who had been marauding and raiding on the Kansas frontier and along the Arkansas route, into moving to Indian reservations.

Custer set out from Fort Riley with his force of Seventh Cavalry to Fort Harker, a distance of ninety miles, where his command was strengthened by another two troops of cavalry. He then pushed on to Fort Larned on the Arkansas River, seventy miles to the south-east, where Hancock had agreed to halt the expedition while a council with the Indians took place. It was not far from the fort that Custer and his men had their first sight of the awesome battle array of the well armed Plains Indians. A clash between Hancock's force and the Indians seemed imminent but the Indians parleyed, claiming they wished for peace. Perhaps Hancock was reluctant to join battle there and then with such a formidable Indian force and when the Indians agreed that the soldiers could continue their march through their village and the chiefs would meet later at General Hancock's headquarters for a broader discussion, Hancock was agreeable. However, the majority of the Indians decided it would be best for them to abandon their village and retreat. The army took up the pursuit.

Custer and his men were subsequently involved in several brushes with hostile Indians but there was no opportunity for any spectacular cavalry charge and the frustrating campaign fizzled out. However, it was decided that Custer should reconnoitre the country from Fort Hays, near the Smoky Hill River, to Fort McPherson on the Platte, proceed to Fort Sedgwick to replenish supplies, go south to Fort Wallace and then back to Fort Hays.

In June the expedition left Fort Hays under Colonel Wickliffe Cooper, the second-in-command. Wickliffe Cooper, a heavy drinker and one of the leading

16

lights in the officer faction opposed to Custer, committed suicide at Medicine Lodge Creek on June 8. Custer had been living with Libbie at Fort Hays and it was in his nature to stay with her to the last minute. He told Wickliffe Cooper to camp eighteen miles ahead while he stayed behind to arrange last minute details and he would catch him up before the start of the second day's march.

Near the Republican River a party of Indians, comprising a hundred or more mounted warriors, was seen. A squadron was sent in pursuit but failed to over-haul the swift Indian ponies. The march continued with Will Comstock, the young white guide, scouting for Custer. Comstock was familiar with the terrain and with the ways of Indians and was able to speak several Indian languages. Custer thought highly of him and attributed the relatively easy approach of the column to Fort McPherson, where he met General Sherman, to Comstock's ability as a guide.

From the Platte, Custer moved due south in his search for Indians. The cavalrymen picked their way cross country for several uneventful days and finally found themselves back on the Republican where they set up camp between Fort Sedgwick, seventy miles to the east, and Fort Wallace, about the same distance to the north-east. Sherman had instructed Custer to go to Fort Sedgwick where he would then be, but Custer decided to change the plan.

While Custer had been at Fort McPherson, under the impression that after completion of the expedition he would be staying at Fort Wallace for several weeks, he had written to his wife at Fort Hays asking her to meet him at Fort Wallace. Now, instead of turning north to Fort Sedgwick he decided just to send an officer and escort to receive despatches and carry a despatch to General Sherman telling him that he proposed to continue with his forces on a march of thirty days or more; that supplies would be needed and, as the country between the camp on the Republican and Fort Wallace was more suitable for wagons than that between the camp and Fort Sedgwick, a wagon train and escort would go to Fort Wallace for supplies, scheduled to return at the same time as the despatches. Major Joel Elliott left for Fort Sedgwick on June 23, the same day as Colonel West and a full squadron of cavalry escorting a wagon train in the charge of Colonel Cooke headed toward Fort Wallace.

When he sent off the wagon train from his camp on the Republican River, Custer expected that Libbie had already arrived at Fort Wallace and he sent a letter to her with Cooke telling her to come to the Republic Camp under Cooke's escort. So anxious was Custer for a reunion with his wife that he was prepared to let her risk the dangerous journey through hostile territory. The extent of the appalling danger to which the randy Custer was prepared to expose Libbie was evident that very night. The Indians attacked, intending to take the camp by surprise, but a picket, although wounded, sounded the alarm. Custer was alerted by his brother Tom. The cavalrymen drove back the Indians and, after Custer had parleyed with them in an attempt to discover their intentions in the area, they made off. Another party of Indians was reported in the direction in which Major Elliott had departed. Captain Hamilton and his troop, sent to reconnoitre, had a sharp encounter with hostiles and Custer began to have fears for Elliott, but Elliott and his detachment finally returned safely on June 27.

Custer's anxiety about the wagon train had been growing and with plenty of reason. It could hardly be supposed that Indian scouts had not detected the movement of the wagons and it was more than likely they would attack the train on its return journey to the Republican River when it would be laden. With this on his mind and the thought of Libbie on her way to join him, Custer sent a squadron under Colonel Myers to join Colonel West and the part of the escort encamped halfway to Fort Wallace and wait there with him for the wagon train to escort it back to the Republican River.

But the wagon train was only half way back to the camp where Colonel West was waiting with the escort when Comstock spotted hostile Indians. Colonel Cooke and Lieutenant Robbins organised the train for mobile defence and proceeded ready to meet the anticipated Indian attack. They did not have to wait long. The Indians, presenting a terrifying picture, came whooping and yelling down the slopes. The cavalrymen poured a volley into them from their Spencer carbines as the circling Indians came in close, forcing them to veer away sharply and draw off. The Indians soon attacked again. This time over six-hundred painted warriors came riding furiously in a wide circle round the train, gradually closing in and firing as they rode. But the train inexorably continued its journey throughout the attack which lasted three hours. The

Indians finally broke off the engagement as Colonel West's detachment was in sight, and the wagons rolled on to the camp on the Republican River. Libbie was not with the train. The message sent to her by Custer from Fort McPherson had not reached her and she was still at Fort Hays.

Custer then struck north toward the Riverside camp on the Platte as directed in despatches from Sherman, delivered by Elliott to Custer. It was learned there that the Indians had attacked the stage coach nearest the camp the previous

evening. Custer was able to telegraph to Fort Sedgwick asking for further instructions and received a surprising reply saying that the day after Elliott had left the Fort a second detachment, ten troopers of the Second Cavalry under the command of Lieutenant Kidder and guided by a famous Sioux chief, Red Beard, had left with important despatches for Custer from Sherman, with orders to proceed to Custer's camp near the forks on the Republican River and, if Custer had already left, to follow his trail. Custer asked for copies of the despatches Kidder had carried, as the Lieutenant had not shown up. The orders were for Custer to strike south across country to Fort Wallace on the Smoky Hill River. Custer decided to move directly to Fort Wallace owing to the low state of his supplies, and hoped to run into traces of Kidder and his party, but the fact that Fort Hays and Libbie were not too far from Fort Wallace no doubt influenced Custer to make this decision.

The troopers for a long time had been dissatisfied with the quality and paucity of their rations. Graft and corruption among traders and suppliers to the commissaries of military posts were mainly to blame. Moreover, the soldiers were disgruntled with marching and counter-marching through hostile Indian country, with experience of the ferocity of Indians and the risk of torture and mutilations to be suffered at their hands if captured, and all for a pittance. The soldier Custer was a hard taskmaster. He knew discipline in the field was essential and in a mainly guerilla war such as the Indians fought it was vital that every man concentrated on the task for which he had enlisted.

However, on the Platte, Custer's men found themselves near the main line of overland travel to the newly discovered goldfields and the chance of earning high wages as miners, the prospect of good ancillary jobs in mining towns and the off-chance of striking gold themselves, was a temptation to the disillusioned soldiers. For a man who had to face death and hardship, deprivations, lack of freedom and the absence of women for a few dollars a week the lure was difficult to ignore.

As it was, desertion in the U.S. Army was endemic, especially among the troops along the Western frontier. Inducements to stay in the Army were negligible, pay and food were poor, petty restrictions and useless drills irked the men, there was little entertainment and opportunity for leisure, and life in the far-flung army posts and forts was dull, monotonous and lonely. Furthermore, as is usual in most armies, there was a vast visible gap in the different life styles provided for officers and enlisted men, and this applied particularly to their womenfolk, where wives were allowed in the larger posts.

A lot of junior officers were career men who would have been of very little account as civilians and knew little and cared less about soldiering and the men they commanded, bolstering their egoes with punctiliousness in trifling details, drills and inspections. The officers were mostly concerned with the benefits of being officers; few earned the respect of their men.

Punishment of six months or a year for desertion was no deterrent, although on active service the punishment could be death. A man might join the army to

General Tucumseh Sherman, the Army commander, in Napoleonic pose.

be clothed and fed but after a while, when his belly was full and winter was past, he would take the road to freedom, not worrying too much about a few months in prison if he were caught. At least in prison he would not be shot at by bloodthirsty Indians.

21

Custer (centre) bags a bear on a hunting expedition.

On the morning of departure from the Platte, orders for the move having been given the evening before, over forty men were reported to have deserted during the night. Now forty men do not suddenly make up their minds to take off at the same time. They must have discussed the matter and agreed to desert en masse.

Custer was often accused of a lack of sensitivity in his dealings with his men and a disregard for their welfare. It is likely that Custer had contempt for their ignorance, ineptitude, recalcitrance, slovenliness in their personal habits and quarrelsomeness, yet he went out on a limb if he thought they were being cheated. Custer was a soldier and he wanted his men to be soldiers. However, it was a fact that Custer looked to his own comfort and made the most of his leisure time for recreation and hobbies. He saw no reason why he should not take advantage of his position as a commanding officer to attend to his own welfare. Custer saw to it that he had every comfort that was possible, even under difficult circumstances. He saw no reason why he should not see his wife at every opportunity; that his men were limited in their sex lives was no reason why he should be so limited, even if it meant taking French leave or bending rules, and he never let the thought of punishment deter him. An absentee at times, perhaps he may have been, but a deserter never, for Custer was always ready to take the field against the enemy whenever called upon. He never shirked or tried to duck a fight. Custer could not count on the loyal support of all his officers for his decisions. He had to contend with jealousy, pettiness and constant sniping at his authority and it was necessary for him to deal firmly with insubordination as he saw fit.

In the field, with Custer, the business of soldiering was paramount and the desertion of forty men when every man counted, in territory infested with hostile

Indians, was no light matter. When Custer left the Platte he was forty men short and the possibility of more desertions must have worried him a good deal.

The column started off at daylight and at noon halted to rest, having marched fifteen miles. The men thought that the march would not be resumed until the next day, but orders were given to resume the march after one hour. As preparations were being made to move, seven men were seen galloping off back along the trail with another seven men on foot following in their wake. Custer ordered a detachment in pursuit of the deserters with instructions to bring them back dead or alive. Drastic measures had to be seen to be taken to discourage further desertions. The rot had to be stopped. Any officer in the field who failed to do otherwise under similar circumstances and so jeopardised his command in hostile territory would have been court-martialled for dereliction of duty. It was hard on the deserters, but they had had no qualms about leaving their comrades in the lurch.

The mounted deserters had no difficulty in getting away but the men on foot were soon within hailing distance and Major Joel Elliott, senior officer in charge of the detachment in pursuit, called on them to halt and surrender. The deserters ignored the call and kept going until they were overtaken and were again called on to surrender. One of the fugitives, it was alleged, raised his carbine and the officers in charge of the pursuit, in no mood to put themselves and their men at risk for a bunch of deserters, promptly opened fire. Three of the deserters fell wounded and the others gave up. One of the wounded died later. Benteen's account of the incident was lurid and, as usual, critical of Custer. He said that the men were shot down by Elliott, in accordance with Custer's instructions, while begging for their lives, but as Benteen had not been present at the incident that statement was either an invention or was based on hearsay. The deserters would, naturally, be inclined to give a biased version of the incident, and the troopers who had taken part in the pursuit would more likely be sympathetic toward their fellow soldiers and side with them rather than with their officers, especially when the troopers might themselves have been contemplating desertion at some time or other. Benteen piled on the agony in later statements, making Custer the villain of the piece and the deserters the heroes. However, whatever the rights and wrongs of the incident, Custer was the commanding officer at the time, and if he thought draconian methods were necessary to halt a degenerating situation at a critical time, the decision was his.

The march to Fort Wallace continued and guide Comstock and his Delaware scouts picked up the trail of the missing Kidder detachment and eventually came upon what was left of it. It was a revolting scene. Every man had been stripped, hacked and mutilated beyond recognition, and all had been scalped. Their putrefying bodies were pierced with dozens of arrows and there was evidence that some of them had been tortured with fire. It was a sobering sight for Custer's men. The butchered troopers were buried in a common grave before Custer continued his march.

The next evening, Custer reached Fort Wallace where he learned that the

The fate of Lieutenant Kidder and his party.

fort had been attacked by Indians twice within the past few days and was virtually cut off; that many stage stations on the Smoky Hill route had been abandoned and the fort had been without mail or despatches for some time. Furthermore, supplies were low and as Custer was expected to use the fort as a base for further operations he decided to break through hostile territory to Fort Hays, then on to Fort Harker, the nearest supply depot, with a picked band of troopers riding fast horses. No doubt, the thought that his wife was in Fort Hays was on Custer's mind when he decided to lead the detachment to get supplies. He was not the sort of man to miss an opportunity to see his wife.

Custer rode his men hard through territory full of marauding Indians and, pausing to rest at Downer's Station, garrisoned by a small detachment of infantry, was there waiting when a party of stragglers rode in and reported that they had been attacked by a few dozen Indians, losing two men. Custer decided to push on at once and reached Fort Hays, having covered the distance of one hundred and fifty miles from Fort Wallace in fifty-five hours, a fast rate of travel but well within the range of picked men riding picked horses.

At Fort Hays, Custer was disappointed to learn that Libbie had gone to Fort Riley, sixty miles beyond Fort Harker. He then decided to go on to Fort Harker with just his brother Tom, Colonel Cooke and two troopers, leaving Hamilton with the remainder of the men to rest for a day and then follow on to Fort Harker, by which time Custer would have made arrangements for a supply train to be got ready for Fort Wallace. Ostensibly Custer's idea was to expedite the procedure, but it is more likely that he was anxious to see Libbie and was scheming for a chance to go on to Fort Riley to meet her. Complaints were later made that Custer had pushed his men to the limit of endurance to Fort Hays, yet Custer and his four picked men went on to cover the distance of sixty miles

Indian scout. Sketch by the author from an old drawing.

Robert Shaw as Custer,
looking very much like Errol
Flynn as Custer.

Charge! Scene from *Custer of the West*, with Robert Shaw. (National Screen Services Ltd.)

to Fort Harker in less than twelve hours without rest. Custer never seemed to think that his troopers might not be capable of doing what he could do. Most of his men were evidently nowhere near as fit as he.

At Fort Harker, Custer made a full report of his operations to General Andrew J. Smith who was in command of the military district and, as this was the first telegraph station he had encountered since having discovered the bodies of Kidder and his party, Custer took the opportunity to telegraph the information to Fort Sedgwick. Then, having arranged for supplies to be drawn, and believing that he had sewn up the situation neatly, Custer saw no necessity to wait around in Fort Harker for the train to be loaded and made ready to leave, and there was time for him to go on to see Libbie at Fort Riley, only ninety miles away by rail. Custer maintained that he applied for authority to do this and received it. Whether he did or not could not be proved, but Custer was determined to see Libbie and did.

In September a court-martial was convened by General Hancock to try Custer on seven charges. Among the charges were that he had absented himself from Fort Wallace and proceeded to Fort Riley without proper authority, and that he had ordered his men to make a rapid march from Fort Wallace to Fort Hays with tired and unfit horses. But Custer and his small party had ridden miles further than any of the other men, and with less rest, without being any the worse for it.

There were some men who contended that Custer had deserted his command at Fort Wallace in the same way as the men had deserted on the Platte and for which they had been punished. The analogy is absurd. Custer left his men at Fort Wallace safely esconced with the Fort's garrison. But even were Custer an absentee he never was a deserter. There is a vast difference between a soldier who is ready to take a bit of French leave, something for which he is often admired, and a deserter. A deserter does not intend to return to his unit and is usually not particular about leaving his comrades in the lurch when he decides to take off. Custer's men deserted on the Platte when there was a real prospect of imminent action with the enemy. In any army unit there are also those who, when a man chooses to take French leave, lacking the courage to do likewise are jealous and their condemnations of the absentee, more often than not, are just big bunches of sour grapes. Custer had a beautiful wife and there were men in his regiment who envied him for that.

Another charge against Custer was that at Downer's Station, after the stragglers had reported being attacked, he had taken no action to recover the bodies of the men who had been killed. Risking lives and wasting time to recover the bodies would, perhaps, have been commendable but not very wise, and Custer, after all, was a practical soldier.

Additional charges brought by a Colonel West related to Custer's methods with the deserters on the Platte on July 7, 1867. But Colonel West's motives in bringing the charges were suspect though he was a hardened soldier and an experienced Indian fighter. Perhaps he resented the way he had been used in

25

the episode of Custer's scheme to bring Libbie to the camp on the Republican River. Perhaps he took what he saw as a legitimate opportunity for putting a nail in Custer's coffin; it is even possible he thought that Custer had been too harsh in his discipline. Whatever his real reasons for bringing the charges against him, Custer bore him no malice. In general, Custer's resentment against his detractors and backbiters was never more than transitory and he was always undeterred in going his own sweet way.

Custer was convicted on all the main charges and the fact is that the sentence of one year's suspension of rank and pay, a light sentence in view of the seriousness of the charges, reflects the true impressions of Custer by the court and the underlying reservations about his alleged conduct. As far as the court was concerned, Custer was too good a soldier to bludgeon into the ground.

The Custers spent the rest of autumn and winter at Fort Leavenworth, Kansas, where General Sheridan gave up his own quarters to them, and they spent the spring in their home town of Monroe. It was Sheridan who came to Custer's rescue, requesting that Custer be returned to active duty and that the rest of his sentence be remitted. That Custer was a favourite of Sheridan there is no doubt, most likely because he realised Custer's value as a soldier. Now Sheridan needed him in a winter campaign he was planning against hostile tribes of Indians in 1868. During Custer's enforced inactivity Major Elliott had commanded the Seventh Cavalry as part of General Sulley's expedition against hostile Indians, a campaign notable for Sulley's ineptitude and lackadaisical handling of the operations and the fact that no progress was made at all in pacifying the Southern Plains.

An incredible commentary on Custer's arrest, court-martial, sentence and subsequent events, are in a letter from Benteen to Goldin written on February 12, 1896 in which he was wrong in just about everything, even Custer's sentence and rehabilitation, but Benteen's self-righteousness, smugness and downright brazen effrontery is best illustrated in this passage:

. . . At all events we were free of Custer till autumn of 1868, then by verbal recommendation made by J. Schuyler Crosby, A.A.G. for Sheridan, who came to me from that General, offering me the command of the Seventh Cavalry in the field. Major Elliott and Captain Wm. Thompson, who were my seniors, were to be given leave of absence. I politely but firmly declined the compliment of being so selected, recommending to Colonel Crosby that Sheridan secure the remission of the unexpired portion of Custer's sentence and let him join the command, saying that perhaps he would have, and exhibit, more sense and judgment than he had during his former short tour of command. So Custer came!

"So Custer came!" Benteen certainly excelled himself in that amazing letter. It is difficult to imagine Benteen turning down the command of the Seventh if it were offered to him, and that he suggested that Custer be restored to his command is beyond all belief. His pontifical remarks about Custer's future conduct are pompous and hypocritical and the allusion that Sheridan considered Benteen's judgment and restored Custer to the command of the Seventh Cavalry on his recommendation is evidence of his megalomania.

Indian fighter

SHERIDAN PLANNED HIS CAMPAIGN AGAINST THE PLAINS INDIANS TO BE A bitter one in every sense. The Plains were almost devoid of any natural shelter from piercing icy winds and blizzards, and biting frosts and ice left little grazing for the Indian ponies. It was a time when the nomadic tribes had to draw in their horns and make camp near any form of shelter from the bleak weather where water and timber were available. It was a time when the Indians had to live off the supplies of buffalo they had hunted until the end of autumn; it was a time when cold and hunger sapped the strength of the Indian men, women and children; it was the time of truth when the Indian warriors must have realised that however bravely they struggled against the white intruders their efforts were hopeless and their doom a foregone conclusion. It was the time when their spirit was at its lowest ebb.

Sheridan's plan was to seek out the Indians huddled miserably in their villages, kill as many as possible, slaughter their ponies, burn their stocks of food and fuel, force survivors out into the open where, without food, shelter or transport, they would be left to perish. Sheridan had written to President Grant saying, "We must act with vindictive earnestness against the Sioux, even to their extermination, men, women and children." Before Washita, Sheridan's order to Custer was unequivocal, "Kill or hang all warriors and bring back all women and children."

Grizzled veteran frontiersmen were doubtful about this policy, knowing full well that the Plains in winter were even more unhospitable to would-be invaders than they were to the Indians. The problems of communications, shelter and supplies facing troops in temperatures which dropped below zero would severely strain the resources of any army, and morale in the field, under gruelling conditions and the prospect of a vicious campaign where the soldiers were expected to be callous and brutal to combatants and non-combatants, including women and children, was not likely to be high. It was in the nature of soldiery however that when the chips were down they would take out their resentment on the enemy, men, women and children alike, without too much searching of conscience.

With his usual impatience, as soon as Custer received the telegram from Sheridan about his reinstatement, he left for Fort Hays without waiting for official confirmation, arriving on September 30, 1868 at the new headquarters of General Sheridan. Without delay he went on to rejoin the Seventh Cavalry encamped on Bluff Creek, about thirty miles from Fort Dodge. He arrived there on October 5 to find the men demoralised from the effects of their debilitating and ineffective operations under General Sulley and some of the officers, especially those who had ganged up on Custer at his court-martial, more than apprehensive about Custer's likely attitude toward them. However, as was customary with Custer, he showed no vindictiveness and no desire for revenge; his main concern was, as a soldier, to prepare at once for the campaign that promised to be a hard one. A new depot, called Camp Supply, was set up as a base for military operations, to which Sheridan moved his field headquarters.

On the morning of November 23, 1868, in blinding snow, Custer and eleven troops of the Seventh Cavalry moved off on the big hunt for Indians. Night came when the column was fifteen miles from the post and camp was set up while the snow continued unabatingly. Four days later, riding through snow and slush the troopers reached the frozen Canadian River where the shivering men and horses paused. Custer sent Major Joel Elliott up-river to reconnoitre while the men set to work breaking the surface ice on the river to ford across. Elliott sent back a messenger to Custer saying he had found an Indian trail leading to the Washita River. Custer sent back a reply to Elliott instructing him to continue the reconnaissance along the trail until 8 p.m., then wait for the Seventh to catch up, and this they did. They rested, had a hot drink and something to eat before moving off again in moonlight, with a couple of Osage scouts scouting ahead, until finally, from the crest of a hill, they saw an Indian village of some seventy lodges stretched below along the banks of the Washita River. It was the Cheyenne village of Chief Black Kettle, who had been peaceably disposed to whites at one time, and who had survived a previous attack on an Indian village which believed itself to be under white protection.

Custer decided to attack the village at dawn from four sides and accordingly split his force of eight hundred men into four detachments under the commands of Major Elliott, Colonel Thompson, Colonel Myers and himself, with Colonel Cooke and his sharpshooters included in his own detachment, and Colonel West in command of one squadron and Captain Hamilton in charge of the other.

The deployment of the troops continued through the intensely cold night in freezing snow. Then came the painful wait by men numb with cold, fitfully snatching sleep huddled together for warmth in knots of four or five, close to their shivering horses. It was a night when further reconnaissance was impossible. Of course, later came the inevitable nit-picking from Benteen who claimed that while the men froze, Custer was comfortable, wrapped in warm buffalo robes in a tent. Perhaps Custer should have chosen to freeze with his men or allowed them to share his tent, all two-hundred of them.

Custer's orders from Sheridan were to attack Indian villages and here was Custer poised over a large sleeping village in a position to strike a stunning exemplary blow at the enemy. Custer, the soldier, was not a man to hesitate in

Wolf Robe, a typical
Cheyenne.

Phil Sheridan, hero of the
Civil War and implacable
enemy of the Indian. He
favoured Custer.

such circumstances. The advantages from a military point of view were all in his favour. The probability of taking the enemy by surprise with his four-pronged attack was almost certain and the chances of heavy casualties to his troops therefore unlikely.

In the pale light of dawn filtering through freezing mist, the cavalrymen moved slowly down into the valley like grey ghosts. They were tense and sweating despite the cold as they rode toward the woods on the edge of the Indian village, accoutrements rattling, horses snorting jets of steam as they walked warily over brittle bracken and frosty fronds, hooves muffled by snow. Then a rifle shot with a ringing ricochet of sudden sound broke the tension. Custer yelled an order for the band to break into the stirring regimental march *Garry Owen*, which was greeted with cheers and shouts from the other detachments closing in on the village. The bugles sounded the charge and the Seventh Cavalry galloped furiously into action.

The troopers swept into the village firing into the lodges and cutting down whoever emerged. There was no chance of distinguishing young from old, men from women or even children in the poor light, the blaze of passion and excitement and the pandemonium of wildly cavorting horses, cursing soldiers, yelling Indians and screaming children. Cheyennes made for the freezing river intent on using the embankment for cover. Others fired from behind trees and stacks of timber. Some women and children were escorted downstream to safety by a few older men as the warriors made a desperate stand to beat off the cavalry attack. But Black Kettle's village was not the only Indian village in the vicinity and the noise of the battle had alerted neighbouring Indians and parties of scouts began to appear along the river.

Custer realised the danger and lost no time in mopping up the village. Then he grimly proceeded to carry out the rest of Sheridan's orders. The Indian ponies – according to Benteen eight hundred of them – were slaughtered and the tepees and their contents fired. One hundred and five Indians had been killed and fifty-three women and children captured against a loss of six soldiers killed, including Captain Hamilton, son of General Hamilton, and several wounded, a very neat operation from the military point of view. But Elliott, operating in his given sector during the lightning attack, had apparently gone in pursuit with eighteen troopers of a band of fleeing warriors and had been cut off.

When Custer heard that Elliott and the troopers were missing he sent out search parties up to two miles in the direction where Elliott had last been seen, but nothing was found and there was Custer with his cold, battle weary men and sullen prisoners, surrounded by increasing numbers of hostile and revengeful Indians arriving from other villages. Custer came in for a lot of criticism, especially from Benteen, for allegedly abandoning Elliott and his party without having made a thorough search for them.

A letter to DeGresse, published in the *New York Times* on February 14, 1869, which was anonymous but which Benteen was later stung into admitting having

Little Raven, head
chief of the Arapahoes.

written, was a lurid and tear-jerking exercise. He snidely suggested that Custer had left Elliott to his fate, being preoccupied in the sadistic pleasure of slaughtering horses when he should have been risking time and men in failing light to continue the search for Elliott even though the Indians were known to be mustering in dangerous numbers. Benteen shed crocodile tears for the dead women and children, the "crowd of frightened, captured squaws and papooses," and seemed to imply that Custer shot the ponies, all eight-hundred of them, singlehanded.

There is no argument against the fact that the Battle of Washita resulted in a massacre of Indians taken by surprise and the massacre of Elliott and his men in ambush, but Benteen must have known that the very nature of the campaign and the stern orders of Sheridan would result in extreme situations and he was being less than honest in his criticisms of Custer's conduct in the campaign. Benteen knew that casualties inflicted on the Indians in surprise attacks on their villages would be indiscriminate, just as a preliminary artillery bombardment would have been.

Custer was also criticised over the battle by General W. B. Hazen, superintendent of the Southern Indian District, who maintained that Black Kettle was a peaceful man, yet the raid on his village revealed evidence of raids by his people on Kansan settlers. It is possible that from time to time Black Kettle had found it politic to maintain peace on the frontier. Indian agent A. G. Browne remarked of Black Kettle that, "He was a good man; he was my friend and he was murdered." However, a soldier on a punitive expedition with explicit instructions could hardly be expected to announce his arrival in a village in hostile country and ask for the chief's credentials.

Custer might have shown a lack of humanitarianism if it interfered with his duty as a soldier, but whereas this lack of sentiment is a flaw in the character of a civilian it can be an asset to a campaigning soldier. Custer had seen more than a fair share of the waste and wanton destruction of so called civilised warfare, as well as the particular cruelties of the Indian wars with the tortures, scalpings and mutilations, and was as immune to the sight of blood and carnage as any seasoned soldier would be. All the same, that Custer did have compassion is evident in his writings.

Custer's view of the Indians was a soldier's assessment. He admired their courage, fortitude, horsemanship and fighting prowess, but he was under no illusions about their diabolical cruelty, their abysmal ignorance, duplicity and natural antipathy to the white stealers of their lands. Realistically he faced the fact that the Indians were never going to submit willingly to what amounted to their complete subjugation, and only bitter fighting and inhumane treatment could eventually break their will to resist the encroachments of the whites. Custer was a sharp tool used by a relentless white government to whittle away the red man's power and, at Washita, Custer inflicted a deep cut in the framework of Indian society.

Whatever controversy arose over Washita there is little doubt that Sheridan

Sharp Nose, typical member of the Arapaho tribe.

was well pleased with the issue and so was Sherman, his superior, who sent his congratulations. As a military operation the success of Washita can be judged from the pattern it set for subsequent actions against the Indians on the Plains, which finally destroyed their power completely.

After the battle Custer returned with his men to Camp Supply where he paraded with his men in a colourful victory ceremony before Sheridan. The Indian prisoners taken back to the camp by the Seventh Cavalry included a twenty-year-old Cheyenne girl, Monahseeta, whom Custer favoured and the inevitable rumours spread that the girl had become his mistress and later bore him a son. It soon became common gossip among the personnel in the cramped circle of frontier army camps. Whether Custer had a mistress and a half-breed son or not was nothing that reflected on his ability or his competence as a fighting soldier. It was just another twig to add to the birch to beat Custer with.

Custer and his men were not kept idle for long. Sheridan sent them off again to round up hostile Indians in Oklahoma and force them into government reservations. With the Seventh Cavalry went twelve companies of the Nineteenth Kansan Volunteer Cavalry under the command of Colonel Samuel J. Crawford. The Kansans were keen to avenge attacks made by Indians on Kansan settlements and wagon trains and they were glad to take part in the operations against hostile Cheyennes, Kiowas and Arapahoes.

The ultimate destination of the expedition was Fort Cobb and, as General Sheridan wished to transfer his field headquarters there, he decided to accompany the expedition, taking the opportunity to avail himself of the formidable escort, but he waived any right to exercise command. The entire force left Camp Supply on the morning of December 7 and moved toward the Washita. There, Custer and Sheridan deployed a hundred troopers to search the terrain near the battlefield to try to ascertain the fate of Elliott and his party. Their bodies were found two miles away from the place where they had last been seen. The corpses were lying in a tight circle and it was obvious that the party, cut off and surrounded by hostile Indians, had dismounted to fight a last desperate engagement in which all had been killed and then horribly hacked and savagely mutilated. It was also found that Black Kettle's village had been part of a continuous settlement of Indian villages of Arapahoes, Kiowas and bands of Cheyennes, Comanches and Apache, a veritable hornets' nest and it had been wise for Custer to withdraw from the Washita when he did. It was obvious that he had been quick to assess the danger to his force when he had spotted the hostile Indians arriving on the fringes of his position after the Washita battle. Only his rapid assessment of the threat to his entire force made him cut short the search for Elliott and his detachment. Custer could not be accused of cowardice or a lack of compassion on this score.

In the abandoned Indian lodges much evidence was found of the hasty retreat of the Indians, as well as evidence of Indian atrocities. In the context of Sheridan's plans and the scope of government policy, Washita had been well justified. The next day the command continued along the Indian trail, toward

34

Fort Cobb and on the morning of December 17 Custer's Osage scouts reported that a party of Indians bearing a flag of truce were just ahead. However, before action could be taken a scout from Fort Cobb arrived with a message from General W. B. Hazen, Commander of the Southern Indian District, which stated categorically that the Indians were friendly and none of them had been on the warpath that season. Custer had plenty of evidence which proved otherwise. Nevertheless, he accepted Hazen's assurances, albeit with reservations. Sheridan was later to express his opinion that Hazen had been wrong and had Custer gone ahead and brought the Indians to task there and then a lot of trouble later could have been averted.

Custer persisted doggedly in his task of getting the recalcitrant Indians back to the reservations. He experienced little trouble with the Arapahoes but he needed to take extreme measures with the Kiowas, arresting their chiefs, Lone Wolf and the murderous Santanta, and threatening to hang them if their followers refused to co-operate. In the case of Chief Stone Forehead of the Cheyennes, Custer displayed his resoluteness and swift summing up of a tricky situation.

In the Cheyenne village of Stone Forehead two white women, taken prisoner in raids on Kansan settlements, were being held. Without hesitation, Custer seized four of Stone Forehead's chiefs as hostages against the return of the women. Custer smoked the pipe of peace with the Indian chief and it was agreed that Stone Forehead and his followers would go peaceably into a reservation. From this pow-wow arose the inevitable legend. According to Indian accounts the medicine man tapped the ashes from the peace pipe on to Custer's left boot, a sign of bad luck for Custer if he broke his word, but this apocryphal story is typical of shrewd medicine men whose solemn pronouncements were made with hindsight rather than foresight.

The Kansans accompanying the expedition admired the way Custer had accomplished the freeing of the captive women without bloodshed. He had shown courage, tact and diplomacy. The Kansans maintained that Custer was popular with his troops and were proud of his achievements.

The Seventh Cavalry returned to Fort Hays, Kansas, to spend the summer and settled down to the routine life of a military establishment. Custer was able to indulge in his hobbies which included hunting, taxidermy, writing and amateur theatricals. The Seventh Cavalry still carried out sorties in the region but the assignments consisted mainly of unspectacular escort and scouting duties. Custer was happy to relax with his wife as far as his duties, which were not onerous at the time, allowed.

Then in March 1871 the regiment was moved down south to the states of what had been part of the Confederacy and broken up into detachments to police the area and help enforce the laws of the internal revenue. Custer, with two companies of the regiment, went to Elizabethtown where the Ku Klux Klan had been active. The Klan had been increasing its terrorist attacks from 1868 and Grant had got Congress in 1871 to enact legislation to repress the lawlessness

35

in the south with force.

However, for the next two years, life for General Custer and his troops was quiet after the experiences of the Indian campaigns and once again Custer and his wife were able to relax, Custer interesting himself with his usual hobbies and horse racing, but also able to settle down to some serious writing. He started a series of articles for *The Galaxy*, a 'quality' magazine, which were later published as a book under the title *My Life on the Plains*.

The narrative was, for the most part, a romantic idealised account of life on the Frontier. It was a soldier's adventure story. Custer did not dwell on the horrors and sufferings of war but rather on the inspiring panoramic breadth of scene, the larger-than-life characters, the colourful costumes and customs of the Indians, and the picturesque dress and language of white scouts. Those were the things that really appealed to Custer. Indian fighting was a duty which he carried out efficiently without fear. Though he would react to the excitement and experience at the time, it was not what he really wished to do most, and war was incidental to his narrative. Yet the excitement and feel of the period is in every page. The book shows Custer as a keen observer of all that went on around him. It shows him as a typical soldier, able to find a bright side to most unpleasant situations and to look back on pleasant experiences rather than on the sordid.

Custer did not hesitate to court a certain amount of unpopularity by stating his views on the baser side of the characters of many Indians and the blindness of many military men and agents in their dealings with them. He specifically criticised General Hazen for having been taken in by the Indians over Washita and referred to the letter Hazen had written to him about the friendly attitude of the Kiowas, but without rancour.

In January 1872 Custer was detailed to leave Elizabethtown and escort the Grand Duke Alexis of Russia on a buffalo hunt. Accompanying the party was another favourite of Sheridan, William F. (Buffalo Bill) Cody, the famous frontier scout who, during the campaign of 1868, had reconnoitred the route from Fort Larned to Fort Hays and onward to Fort Dodge through territory infested with hostile Indians. He had brought back valuable information for General Sheridan about the location of Cheyenne winter settlements.

Like Custer, Cody was a colourful character and expert buffalo hunter. The press had given him too a good deal of coverage and it was, no doubt, very gratifying to the Grand Duke to have two such universally known frontiersmen to escort him. It was understandable that the press would see good copy in the excursion and further publicise and add to the prestige of the two dashing American heroes, who for the public epitomised the romantic wild west.

Another probable reason why Custer was chosen to accompany the Grand Duke was because of his culture and breadth of interests. He and Libbie entertained the Russian Duke in Louisville and accompanied him down river to New Orleans. There were many high-ranking officers' wives who must have

A thorn in Sherman's side –
Santana, second chief of the
Kiowas.

envied them and had had a thing or two to say about it to their husbands.

Meanwhile, in Dakota the Sioux were becoming increasingly recalcitrant and in February 1873, at the specific order of Sheridan, the Seventh Cavalry was reassembled for service on the Plains. Two troops of the Seventh were placed under the command of Colonel Samuel D. Sturgis with the regimental headquarters at Fort Snelling, Minnesota, and the remaining ten troops under Custer went by rail to Yankton, Dakota Territory, from where they marched to Fort Rice, reaching it on June 10.

Ten days later, as part of the Yellowstone expedition under General David S. Stanley, Custer led his men as an escort for surveyors of the Northern Pacific Railway seeking a northern rail route through Dakota and Montana. The expedition moved up the Yellowstone River and Custer took the opportunity to collect fossils to send back to the University of Michigan. He hunted with his dogs and shot an elk which he stuffed and sent back to the Audubon Club in Detroit.

On August 4, at the mouth of the Tongue River, Custer encountered hostile Indians, but the wily Indian fighter did not fall into a trap set by them. Describing the battle, Custer referred to a similar ambush in which Colonel William Fetterman and eighty-one men had been surrounded and massacred. On August 11 Custer had another brush with the Indians, incurring a few casualties. The expedition eventually made the return journey through difficult country by way of the Musselshell Hills, and Custer came through without losing a single wagon.

Stanley, the commander of the expedition, resented his youthful cavalry commander referring to him as a "cold blooded, untruthful and unprincipled man." He went on to say that Custer was universally despised by all the officers of his regiment excepting his relatives and one or two sycophants, and that he

Custer's home at Fort Abraham Lincoln in Dakota.

had brought a trader into the field without permission, carried an old Negro woman and a cast-iron cooking stove, and delayed the march by his extensive packing in the morning.

But it was not unusual for jealous officers to criticise Custer and indulge in nit-picking. After all, Custer was again drawing newspaper and magazine publicity and many officers had read a lot about Custer even if they had not met him and were conversant with the accounts of Washita and Benteen's spiteful version. Stanley's assessment of the relationship between Custer and his men seems to be based on hearsay and prejudice while his splenetic reference to the Negro woman and iron stove can hardly be considered seriously as criticism of Custer, savouring more of another of those apocryphal stories that abounded about the popular young general during his lifetime and multiplied after his death.

In the autumn of 1873, at the conclusion of the Yellowstone expedition, the Seventh Cavalry was stationed at the newly built Fort Abraham Lincoln, not far from Bismark, North Dakota, then the north western terminus of the North Pacific Railroad. Detachments were sent to surrounding posts like Fort Totter and Fort Rice, while Custer and his family remained at Fort Abraham Lincoln. The family included Libbie, his brother Tom, his sister Margaret – a competent pianist – and her husband, Lieutenant James Calhoun. They settled down in comfortable quarters to garrison life, passing recreational time with the inevitable card games, piano recitals, parties and reading. But soft living did not soften up Custer. When Sioux raiders drove off with a herd of army mules, Custer himself, at the head of his troopers, pursued them. Custer was ever ready to take offensive military action in accordance with his military duties. It was a happy time for Custer, surrounded by his loved ones, with less chance of friction with the anti-Custer faction whose ringleader, the disgruntled, embittered Benteen, was stationed twenty miles away at Fort Rice and was consequently less of a threatening knife at Custer's back.

Custer in the centre of relatives and friends at Fort Abraham Lincoln. Libbie is seated on Custer's right. Immediately behind him is brother-in-law Fred Calhoun and behind Fred is brother-in-law James Calhoun.

41

Road to Little Big Horn

IN THE SPRING OF 1874 CUSTER LED TEN COMPANIES OF THE SEVENTH CAVALRY with orders to explore the Black Hills, a remote and little known area of the Sioux Reservation in North Dakota, confirmed to them by solemn treaty. Ostensibly Custer's assignment was to survey the possibilities of establishing a protective military post in that region. But for many years greedy prospectors and speculators had cast longing eyes on the unexplored Black Hills where it was rumoured that there were rich gold deposits. The country was only just beginning to recover from the financial crisis of 1873 and the government was looking for a boost to its deflated image. They wanted Custer to confirm the rumours of gold in the hills; it was the idea of the exercise.

With Custer's column went two expert gold prospectors and three newspaper correspondents, and it was inevitable that discovery of the minutest quantities of gold would be exaggerated with government collusion. Custer was later accused of making glowing reports about the discovery of gold in the Black Hills, but the reports could only have emanated from the experts in the first place. For all Custer knew about gold mining the experts could have "salted" the gold and he would have taken their discoveries at face value. The government knew how to extract the utmost from their heroes. The newsmen embellished the stories to their newspapers which gratefully seized upon them to boost their sales and dispel the hitherto gloomy financial news with such encouragingly optimistic headlines as, "Prepare for Lively Times," and "The National Debt to be paid when Custer Returns." Custer had been used.

Custer encountered no hostile Sioux in the Black Hills. Most of the tribes were away in Montana. When the gold rush to the Black Hills started it was the Army who tried to keep the hundreds of frenzied white adventurers under control away from the Indian lands, but it was impossible to hold them back as they trampled over the sacred Indian territory in their lust for gold. Perhaps the cunning Government ploy had gone further than intended. Indian resentment built up and finally culminated in the Battle of the Little Big Horn, the red man's final battle. It was a notable victory for the Indian, his last victory, but a hollow victory nevertheless. It led to acceleration of the so-called pacification in an unequal struggle against the pernicious white invader.

It was as if the Indians had been overawed by the enormity of their achievement, of their having annihilated so large a force of white cavalry; as if the sight of the redoubtable Custer dead in the midst of his fallen comrades had unnerved them and made them realise the consequences of what they had done and the retribution it would surely bring. The biggest concentration of warriors the Indians had ever mustered for battle melted away and never took the field again to try conclusions with a white army. Custer's last stand at the Battle of the Little Big Horn was the defeat that turned into victory.

Back in Fort Abraham Lincoln, Custer basked in the glory of his popularity. He was familiar to the public through newspaper accounts of his exploits, for his writing in *The Galaxy* and his book, *My Life on the Plains*, published in 1874. He was a flamboyant figure, instantly recognisable. Every inch a soldier, he was nearly six-foot tall, wide-shouldered and narrow-hipped with the appearance of a natural athlete. His nose and cheek bones were prominent; his chin perhaps a trifle weak.

When in August 1875 he went on extended leave to New York with Libbie, he was lionised by New York society. It was a time when the romance of the West was already replacing the legends and myths of the Civil War, when the broad horizons of the potential of the United States were looming up and uniting the north and south, helping to heal the wounds of the internecine war of a few years before. Custer and his wife were lavishly entertained by prominent social, business and political leaders. They went to dinners, parties and plays and Custer was able to indulge his interest in the theatre and literature, revelling in the fact that in addition to having attained recognition as an outstanding military figure, he had achieved recognition as a writer. He was called upon to address the Century Society, the leading New York literary society, and the New York Historical Society, and was asked to give a series of lectures in 1876. Custer was able to spend some time at Booth's Theatre where a friend of his, Lawrence Barrett, was playing *Julius Caesar*.

Custer had known Sir Henry Morton Stanley, the explorer, when he had been a newspaper correspondent in the early Indian campaigns before being commissioned in 1869, by James Gordon Bennett, the newspaper publisher, to go to Africa to find the Scottish explorer, David Livingstone. Stanley, appreciating the press value of Custer, had given him a good deal of favourable coverage and now Bennett, when he met Custer in New York, was shrewd enough to elicit from him material with high political potential, especially as 1876 was a Presidential year.

Democrats charged that W. W. Belknap, Secretary of War in the Republican administration of President Ulysses S. Grant, was heavily involved in graft, profiteering from army trading posts with crooked traders, cheating soldiers and Indians. Custer had had personal experience of Belknap's involvement in the trading posts scandals when he had brought to the attention of Belknap the outrageous prices his own men of the Seventh Cavalry had been forced to pay traders on the army posts for goods. The Secretary for War had sided with the traders, arousing Custer's suspicions and disgust.

43

Bennett published a series of scorching articles by a reporter, Ralph Meeker, exposing corruption in Indian agencies, based on information and material supplied by Custer. It was also believed on strong evidence, that Custer himself was the author of an article in *The Herald* called "Belknap's Anaconda" published on March 31, 1876, which branded the Secretary as a grafter. Custer publicly stated that traderships at army posts were sold under a system of graft and that the handling of supplies to Indian agencies was corrupt all the way down from Washington and back again. Belknap resigned but the Democrats pressed for an impeachment trial before the Senate, and Custer was summoned to Washington to testify before Congress.

Appearing before the Committee, Custer, always a Democrat like his father before him, was blunt – too blunt for the Republicans. The evidence he gave against Belknap was said to be hearsay and Custer was unable to offer proof. Bringing his troopers to Washington to testify was not an idea accepted by the committee. Recklessly, Custer accused Orville Grant, the President's brother, of receiving bribes for dispensing favours, but being a forthright soldier and not a lawyer, again he was unable to offer proof, merely shrewd observations and assessments. Nevertheless, his accusations were certainly making it uncomfortable for the administration and, after the Congressional hearings, Custer was summoned to testify at Belknap's trial.

Custer was beginning to realise that he had waded into a sea of mud and was getting out of his depth. He wished he could leave Washington behind him and get back to his regiment in Dakota to prepare to lead a proposed new Indian campaign. It had been eight years since he had fought his last sizeable action, the Battle of Washita. Combat with sword and pistol was more in Custer's line than the dirty in-fighting of politics, yet there were those Democrats who saw in Custer the popular idol, someone who could be boosted as a people's champion and pushed into being their Presidential candidate.

Custer managed to extricate himself from the necessity of appearing at Belknap's trial but President Grant, furious with Custer, was stung into giving orders that the young general be barred from accompanying the proposed expedition, let alone lead it. Custer tried to see Grant but Grant refused to meet him. In desperation, Custer, as he often did in such frustrating circumstances, threw caution to the winds and left Washington without approval from the War Department.

It was no wonder that Grant was enraged by Custer's involvement in the Belknap business and his references to Orville. It was well known that Grant had shown marked nepotism in making government appointments in his first term as President of the United States. He had also had to contend with financial panic due to the gold speculations of Jay Gould and James Fiske. In his second term of office, from 1873, Grant was faced with one of the greatest scandals in American history, that of the Crédit Mobilier of America. Charges of corruption had involved Vice-President Wilson, congressmen and judges. There had also been a scandal involving Government officials. Grant certainly did not want a

Opposite Portrait of Custer used as the frontispiece of Whittaker's *Life of General Custer*, published late in 1876.

44

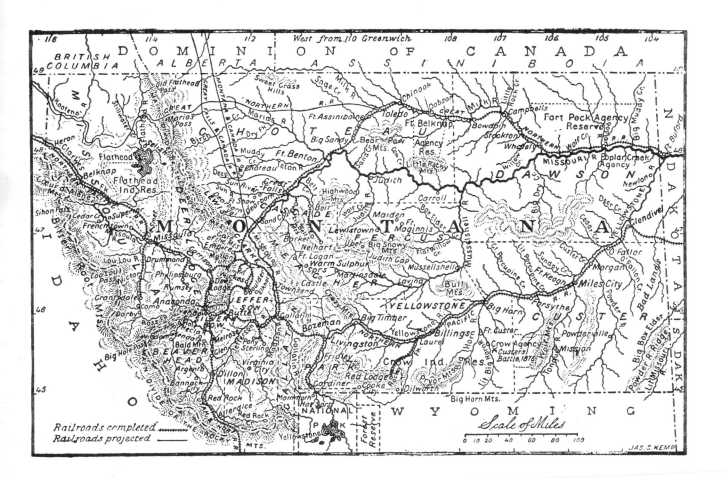

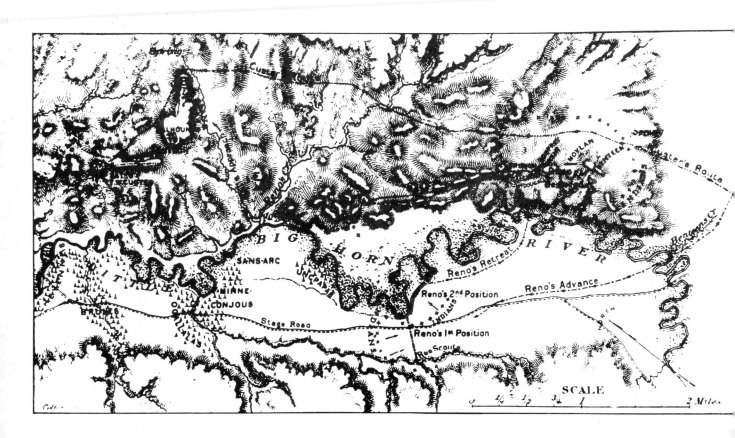

46

Top Map of Montana in 1892.
The site of Custer's battle is
in the Crow Indian
reservation.
Below From the *Century
Magazine* of January 1892,
Godfrey's map of Custer's last
battle.

colourful and popular figure such as Custer to throw his hat into the ring at that time. Custer has often been accused of showing nepotism, but as a Custerphile once remarked, "Some nepotism – giving friends and relations jobs where they get their arses shot off by Indians!"

When Custer arrived in Chicago from Washington under instructions from the Commander of the Army, William Sherman, General Sheridan sent an aide to arrest him, but Sheridan allowed Custer to send telegrams to Sherman pleading his case. Sherman did not reply. Already General Alfred Terry had been appointed to lead the new Indian campaign. At a meeting with Terry in St. Paul, Minnesota, Custer begged him for his help and Terry agreed. He sent a telegram saying that Custer would be, "very valuable with his regiment," and there was no doubt about that, for Terry's practical knowledge of Indian fighting was nil. He also despatched a telegram from Custer to Grant in which Custer passionately, as one soldier to another, requested permission to accompany the expedition, asking to be spared the humiliation of seeing his regiment march off to meet the enemy without him sharing the dangers. Sheridan endorsed the plea and Grant relented.

Grant, his temper cooled, obviously realised the capital that newspapers and friends of Custer could make of his denying the request of a soldier of Custer's calibre to take part in battle. Moreover he must have shrewdly assessed that keeping a disgruntled Custer away from Washington would be best for his beleaguered administration. Of course, Custer might win fresh glory and could become a bigger threat, but on the other hand a dashing soldier like Custer could get himself killed. Either way, that was in the future. In any case, with Custer second-in-command the biggest share of any glory should go to Terry. Custer would not be allowed to get too big for his own boots.

It has been said that immediately it was known that Custer would be going with the expedition after all, there was gossip that Custer had cockily been holding forth that he would find a way to break loose of Terry and run his own way. Apparently the only substantiation for these rumours appeared in an article twenty years after Custer's death, quoting a statement by a Captain Ludlow who claimed that he had been present when Custer had been sounding off, but it is more likely Ludlow's was just another medicine man tale.

Jealousy and envy was in the air around the doomed general as he prepared for the expedition. Brave, confident and undaunted, Custer was determined that there would be newspaper coverage for the expedition, for his part at any rate, and against the advice of Sherman he allowed Mark Kellog, a *New York Herald* reporter, to march with him. Custer had planned previously for press coverage. He had nothing to hide and as a writer he appreciated the wide public interest in the forthcoming campaign and the demand for news. Publicity is a two-edged weapon and it could have worked out adversely for Custer, but that did not worry him.

Sherman's telegram to Terry on the subject was certainly sour. It stated, "Advise Custer to be prudent, not to take along any newspapermen who always

Sioux on the march.

make mischief, and abstain from personalities in the future."

This was typical of high ranking officers who wished to have no eloquent newsmen witness their mistakes, blunders and follies, preferring to make their own either glossy or non-committal reports without risk of comment by a shrewd observer. Furthermore, top ranking generals do not take kindly to subordinates getting the limelight. Sherman, as army chief, was speaking for the main body of his generals.

There is no doubt that newsmen did, as always, latch on to the more colourful characters when covering a campaign; the Montgomerys, Pattons and Rommels are more newsworthy than conventional commanders, and correspondents in Custer's day were just as capable as at any time of puffing up bullfrogs to make good copy. Nevertheless the public wants its vicarious thrills and share of heroes and it is the public who pays the taxes for excursions and wars and the pennies for the papers. Anyway, Custer was no bullfrog.

Grant and Sherman, in granting Custer permission to accompany the expedition, had not done so as any favour to Custer and well he knew it. He had been made to suffer the humiliation of having to beg and plead to fight, to risk his neck and, as it turned out, be killed. Some favour! It was Custer's choice that he go on the fateful expedition. He could not have been seeking glory, particularly. He did not have to "seek the bubble reputation even in the cannon's mouth." His reputation as a fighting soldier was well established. Even had his career terminated as a soldier and even had he not been able to establish himself in politics, he was a knowledgeable and able writer who had already made an impact with his *Life on the Plains*. Publishers would eagerly have vied with each other for his books and he could have made a fat living touring and lecturing.

48

A young successful general with his colour, general appeal, talents and potential
had little to fear from the future. But Custer wanted to be with his regiment
when it went into battle. It was as simple as that.

Sheridan's plan for the campaign against the Sioux was for a three-pronged
attack by three columns, any one of which was thought capable of crushing any
concentration of hostile Indians. General Crook was to head one column from
Fort Fetterman to cut off escape of Indians to the south. General Gibbon was to
bring a column across from Fort Ellis in the west to cut off retreat to the north-
west, while Terry's column from Dakota would come in from the east.

On May 17, 1876 the nine-hundred men of Terry's command left Fort Abraham
Lincoln and marched west to the Powder River which they reached on June 7.
Major Marcus A. Reno, with six troops of the Seventh Cavalry, was sent out
with specific orders to scout the Tongue and the Big Horn rivers but not to
proceed beyond for fear he might alert hostile Indians. Instead of obeying his
instructions, Reno scouted the Rosebud Creek Valley where he came upon a
half-mile wide trail of an Indian village moving up the creek between the
Tongue and the Big Horn rivers. Having already disobeyed his instructions, he
followed the trail for twenty miles. He could then have profited from his original
mistake by seizing the initiative and making a lightning attack on the disorganised retreating Indians, but he chose to turn back to the mouth of the
Tongue River. Custer was furious at the lost opportunity and Terry censured
Reno for his behaviour. It is possible that Reno pushed on toward the Rosebud
after having discovered nothing on the Tongue River, but when he had stum-
bled on such an ominous trail as he did on the Rosebud, and having followed it
for twenty miles, he decided that he had gone far enough. Possibly he had no
wish to compound his disobedience of his orders by risking a fight with the

49

Indians and perhaps jeopardise the overall plan of attack. Reno was not such a man as Custer who would, most likely, have struck while the iron was hot. He would not have hesitated to charge the Indian village as it moved on its cumbersome way.

The consequence of Reno's reconnaissance was Terry's decision to despatch Custer to follow the trail of the Indian village up the Rosebud. On June 21 he issued his orders and directed General Gibbon to march up the Big Horn hoping to catch the retreating Indians between the two columns. Terry's written orders addressed to Custer and signed by the acting Assistant Adjutant were as follows:

"The Brigadier-General Commanding directs that, as soon as your regiment can be made ready for the march, you will proceed up the Rosebud in pursuit of the Indians whose trail was discovered by Major Reno a few days since. It is, of course, impossible to give you any definite instruction in regard to this movement, and were it not impossible to do so, the Department Commander places too much confidence in your zeal, energy and ability to wish to impose on you precise orders which might hamper your action when nearly in contact with the enemy. He will, however, indicate to you his own views of what your action should be, and he desires that you should conform to them unless you shall see sufficient reason for departing from them. He thinks you should proceed up the Rosebud until you ascertain definitely in which direction the trail above spoken of leads. Should it be found (as it appears almost certain that it will be found) to turn towards the Little Horn, he thinks you should still proceed southward, perhaps as far as the headwaters of the Tongue, and then turn toward the Little Horn, feeling constantly however to your left, so as to proclude the probability of escape of the Indians to the south and south-east by passing round your left flank. The column of Colonel Gibbon is now in motion for the mouth of the Big Horn. As soon as it reaches that point it will cross the Yellowstone and move up at least as far as the forks of the Big and Little Horns. Of course its future movements must be controlled by circumstances as they arise, but it is hoped that the Indians, if upon the Little Horn, may be nearly enclosed by the two columns that their escape will be impossible.

"The Department Commander desires that on your way up the Rosebud you should thoroughly examine the upper part of Tullock's Creek, and you should endeavour to send a scout through to Colonel Gibbon's column with information of the result of your examinations. The lower part of the Creek will be examined by a detachment of Colonel Gibbon's command. The supply steamer will be pushed up the Big Horn as far as the forks if the river is navigable for that distance, and the Department Commander, who will accompany the column of Colonel Gibbon, desires you report to him there no later than the expiration of the time for which your troops are rationed, unless in the meantime you receive further orders."

Custer was accused of disobeying these orders. As it turned out he was a most convenient scapegoat, and after the Battle of the Little Big Horn the buzzards were waiting to pounce. Terry's instructions were deemed by most officers after the Little Big Horn to have been explicit. There were not many officers at that time prepared to go against the consensus of high ranking opinions that made Custer the scapegoat, but in many aspects the instructions were equivocal. The preamble to the instructions made optional anything that came later. In the first part of the orders there were no definite instructions; they gave Custer a free hand to play it by ear. Terry indicated his views on what Custer's actions should be and his own thoughts on the subject. His plans for Gibbon were qualified. The most important point in Terry's orders was where he said that he did not wish to impose precise orders which might hamper Custer's actions when nearly in contact with the enemy.

The idea of examining Tullock's Creek in view of Reno's finding the Indian trail on the Rosebud seems to have been a unnecessary swan, and for Terry not to know whether the upper part of the Big Horn was navigable for his steamer is indicative of Terry's incomplete picture of the whole situation. He certainly had no conception of the possibility that any of his columns could be repulsed or defeated. He had not envisaged the repulse of Crook nor the size of the Indian forces. But Terry was no Indian fighter.

Cyrus Townsend Brady, LL.D. in his book *Indian Fights and Fighters* stated: "Every student of military matters knows that the words used, 'He desires that you should conform to them (his own views) unless etc.,' by a military commander conveys a direct positive command." Perhaps. But it would seem that too many commanders issuing important orders use this method of wording in order to hedge their bets so that if anything goes wrong the orders can be interpreted by them in any way it suits them best. Terry wanted Custer on the expedition. He knew Custer's reputation for "going for broke" and banked on him to seize the initiative if he should encounter Indians, but if by any chance Custer should be repulsed – Terry did not contemplate his annihilation – Custer would be the one to "carry the can." Gibbon told Terry that so great had been his fear that Custer's zeal would carry him forward too rapidly that the last thing he had said to him was, "Now Custer, don't be greedy; wait for us." Benteen's version was, "Now don't be greedy, Custer, as there are Indians enough for all of us." Terry elected to accompany Gibbon rather than Custer. He had no wish to inhibit Custer in the field.

There are no mistakes until they are made. The ifs and buts that come afterward are meaningless. The whole pattern of life is a continuing chain reaction. The smallest action is part of the chain. A soldier pausing to tighten a stirrup causes another soldier to halt, altering timing by a fraction of a second that can mean life or death, changing the course of events ad nauseam. It is a useless exercise to go into the ifs and buts after an event. If Crook had not been defeated; if Reno had not wandered on to the trail of the Indian village; if Custer had not been defeated... The actual sequence of events is important but it is impossible to know or understand every factor, every facet, the infinite permutations of links in the chain of each individual action that makes a sequence. The ifs of

51

speculation over any matter is like the old saying, "If my grandmother had had balls, she would have been my grandfather." Or would she?

The question of whether or not Custer disobeyed Terry's orders is immaterial. He interpreted the orders the way he wished; probably the way Terry knew he would. For Custer there could have been no other interpretation. Ludlow's story that Custer had intended disobeying Terry right from the start, although discounted, was without point anyway. It was the way the cookie crumbled.

The prelude to Crook's operations in the south for his co-ordination with Terry's three-pronged offensive against the Sioux, had started several months earlier when General Joseph Reynolds made contact with the enemy, surprising and taking Crazy Horse's village on the Powder River on March 17, 1876. When Crook failed to arrive soon after, it is said Reynolds, under pressure from the Indians, appeared to lose his nerve and retreated so precipitately that a wounded trooper was left behind to the mercy of the Indians. In freezing cold, hard pressed, the troopers had finally run into an irate Crook advancing with the infantry and the wagons. But how precipitate was the retreat in reality? Reynolds had tried to bring away a herd of seven-hundred captured horses which, however, the Indians succeeded in recapturing. It was an ignominious affair and the usual scapegoats were found.

The command was reorganised at Fort Fetterman for the campaign with Gibbon and Terry against the Sioux, but there was never any liason between the three columns. Crook's command was the largest and best equipped single force ever assembled to fight Indians and on May 29, 1876 the column set off, reaching the Tongue River near the Montana boundary line where Crazy Horse, having received news from his scouts of Crook's advance, warned him not to cross the Tongue River and emphasised the warning by opening fire from the bluffs on the other side. After a brief skirmish the Indians retreated.

On June 17, having crossed the Tongue and advanced to the Rosebud, Crook's forces nearly ran into an ambush of thousands of Sioux led by Crazy Horse. In the subsequent fighting, Crows and Shoshones of Crook's force took part. The struggle between the cavalrymen and the Sioux see-sawed across the dusty fields and canyons. Recorded descriptions of the battle are vivid. Rapid sorties, clashing of arms, bloody encounters, charges by the cavalry and counter-charges by the Indians, the fast and furious fire fights, the melees, the continually changing fortunes, the terrible wounds and bravery of Captain Henry have all been described in detail as well as the exploits of Royall, Van Vliet, Noyes and Mills.

But in the final analysis what did it all amount to? Ten soldiers had been killed and twenty-seven seriously wounded. This, out of a force of nine-hundred men which had left camp a few weeks before, seems a comparatively insignificant loss, yet the next day the troops withdrew to their camp at Goose Creek and thereafter were virtually out of the campaign. Crazy Horse had succeeded in neutralising Crook's force and saved his village and was left free to face the forces of Terry and Gibbon, the existence of which he was certainly aware of,

53

Above Arikara scout Red Star.
Below Crow scout White-
Man-Runs-Him.

with disastrous results for Custer.

It was claimed that in the hard fighting Crook had nearly exhausted his ammunition and expended the greater part of his supplies, also that he was encumbered by a large number of wounded. It is strange that such a well pre-pared, well equipped force as Crook's should have expended nearly all its ammunition in the one sustained battle with Crazy Horse and that no fresh supplies were on hand. As for the wounded, provisions should have been made to send them to the rear. If it were Crook's purpose to close the gate to the south against Indians, and this purpose had indeed been achieved in the Battle of the Rosebud, Crook's immediate retirement with Crazy Horse undefeated left the gate wide open again. The sum total of Crook's actions was that nothing had been achieved to help the success of Terry's master plan of the campaign and had, if anything, imbued Crazy Horse with confidence and prejudiced the campaign. Crook's subsequent reconnaissances to probe Crazy Horse's positions were left a little late and were in any case, ineffectual.

At noon on June 22, 1876 the Seventh Cavalry, encamped on the Yellow-stone River, passed in review order before Terry, Custer and Gibbon prior to starting its march up the Rosebud. On the march, besides the six-hundred officers and men of the Seventh were a corps of Arikara and Crow scouts, the Sioux half-blood scout Mitch Bouyer, scout "Lonesome" Charley Reynolds and scout George Herendeen, whose job was to report back to Gibbon the results of scouting Tullock's Creek. Also accompanying the march was the newspaper correspondent, Mark Kellog.

Having covered twelve miles a halt was called at four o'clock that afternoon and in the evening General Custer summoned his officers to a meeting. Custer, it seems, in the knowledge of the stern trials that lay ahead, brisk and business-like, wished to clear the decks for action by trying to dispose of, once and for all, any dissension between himself and his officers and obtain their full co-operation. He stated that he was well aware of criticisms made about him at the head-quarters of the department by certain of his officers and that while he was willing to accept any constructive recommendations at all times from even the most junior officers, it should be done according to regulations. But Benteen, as usual, always ready to quarrel, took exception and, guilty in the knowledge that the cap fitted him, wanted to start another argument with his superior. No doubt to keep the discussion under control, Custer was willing to avoid personalities and, ignoring his insolence, he reassured the bellicose Benteen, but nevertheless rebuked him sharply. In his narrative Benteen did, at least, admit to Custer having given a few good general orders at the meeting as to what should be done by each troop of the regiment in case of attack.

There were those officers who said that Custer now seemed worried and depressed. If that were so it did not show in his letters written to his wife at the time. Custer's officer critics maintained that his manner had always been blunt, peremptory, even brusque. Now they said he had usually been cheerful and confident. Later there would be testimony about Custer's indecisiveness and

Scout Mitch Bouyer.

Curley the scout, a picture by
D. F. Barry a few years after
the Little Big Horn, from the
Denver Public Library
collection.

Right Bloody Knife, the
famous Arikara scout killed
while talking to Reno. *Far
right* another Arikara scout,
Young Hawk.

White Swan, a typical Crow scout.

mental condition before the Battle of the Little Big Horn; more hindsight and nit-picking. But one thing is certain. Custer on that, his last expedition was in peak physical condition, brimful of energy and ready for hard campaigning and battle.

The force marched off early next morning on June 23, and as the day grew hotter clouds of alkaline dust swirled about the tense troopers, parching their throats and irritating their sweating necks. Myriad buffalo gnats swarmed around their faces stinging their dust-filled eyes, while deer-flies tortured the steaming horses. The troopers covered thirty-five rough miles before making camp twelve hours later. That was the awful pace Custer was said to have set. Hardened, seasoned campaigners like the Seventh Cavalry may have grumbled as any soldiers do, but had no more reason to complain than did their general marching with them. None of the troopers thought he was on a routine exercise. There were difficulties. There had been trouble with the pack-trains right from the start. Benteen claimed that he tightened the situation regarding the packs on his own initiative and that later Custer had given his new arrangements his blessing.

The Indian trail was widening with the marks of the poles of the Indian travois ploughing ruts in ground trampled by the hooves of hundreds of ponies. The grass had been cropped close by the feeding herds. On the 24th the troopers

57

covered another twenty-eight miles and the Indian signs became fresher and more ominous. There were the remains of recent meals and of campfires, and the pony droppings had not yet had time to dry. It was evident to all that a vast number of Indians was in close proximity but, as had always been usual at the approach of a large body of troops, was in retreat.

Custer allowed his men to sleep while Crow scouts were sent out to examine the Indian trail more closely. They returned at about 9 p.m. and reported that the trail headed over the divide between the Rosebud and the valley of the Little Big Horn. Custer decided on a night march. He allowed his men to sleep on until 11.30 p.m. and then they set out, covering ten miles toward the crest of the Little Big Horn Mountains, reaching a wooded ravine at 2 a.m. on Sunday where again they rested.

Mitch Bouyer and "Lonesome" Charley Reynolds were as worried as the Arikaras and Crows about the portents of the trail they were following. They knew that more than one tribe of Sioux as well as Cheyennes were on the move. Lieutenant Charles Varnum, commander of the Crow and Arikara scouts, and Bloody Knife, the experienced Arikara scout, warned Custer about clashing with the large body of Indians ahead. Bloody Knife said that there were more Sioux than the soldiers had bullets in their belts, but none realised that Custer's force was outnumbered by as many as five to one. Reynolds, who had scouted the region during the winter and early spring was sure that the Indians were extremely well armed and in a sufficiently belligerent mood to stand and fight instead of adopting their usual tactics of hit and run warfare at which they were adept.

After seven that Sunday morning, Custer, full of fire, rode bareback among the detachments of his troops to tell them to be ready to move off at eight. So the march of Custer's column continued for another ten miles, which was covered in two and a half hours, to a point about fifteen miles from the Little Big Horn. The men were assembled, hidden in a ravine. During the night Lieutenant Varnum and a detachment of his scouts had gone on ahead to a rocky summit from which it was thought the Indian village would be visible; while waiting for the light of dawn Varnum snatched a little sleep. His scouts peered into the night, looking down on the sinuous river twisting through the deep valley below. On the eastern side where the scouts stood, the river was banked by steep bluffs up to one hundred feet high, while on the western side was a flat plain some two miles wide in places. With the light the scouts awakened Varnum, claiming that beyond the plain they could see herds of ponies swarming the hills about twenty miles away, estimating that there were as many as twenty thousand. It is likely that Varnum's fearful Indian scouts exaggerated more than some-what, for keen scout though he was, Varnum could see nothing but the shadows of clouds drifting over the hills. However he reported the observation of the scouts to Custer at about 5 p.m.

During the night march, some badly secured food packs had fallen from the mules and a detail had been sent back to recover them. The detail spotted

Indian scout with lost troop horse; illustration by Frederic Remington.

Photograph of Ogallala, thought to be Chief Crazy Horse.

Indians breaking open a case of hard bread, but the Indians had swiftly taken to their heels. It was obvious that the enemy must now know of the column's presence in the area even had they not known before. It was hardly likely that any body of six hundred soldiers could move through hostile territory without being discovered by Indian scouts.

Custer put the whole force on the alert and the cavalcade moved off at a steady gait. In just over an hour the troopers reached a wooded hollow below the Crow's Nest. As Custer rode on to the observation point the troops fidgeted, loosening the collars of their tunics as the weather was beginning to get warm. Custer, even with his glasses, was no more able to discern the large concentration of ponies that had been reported than had Varnum, but there was no mistaking the size of the huge Indian village stretched out below. Custer returned to the hollow but, soon after, Varnum sent back a runner from the ridge to report to Custer that Indians had been moving downstream suggesting that they were beginning to evacuate the village, the custom usually adopted by hostile tribes under pressure.

As well as the Indians had known of Crook and had discovered Custer, they probably knew about Gibbon. Perhaps they had elected to try conclusions with Custer before he could be reinforced by Gibbon, but in any event Custer was not going to risk their getting away and immediately planned to deal with that contingency. He had to block such a move. He was expecting the arrival of Gibbon from the east and Crook from the south. No attempt had been made to inform Custer of Crook's retreat. He therefore discounted the immediate odds against him. Custer had intended to wait until June 26 to attack, giving more time for Gibbon to appear on the scene with his slow moving force which comprised infantry as well as some artillery, but circumstances had arisen which demanded immediate action. "Push" had come to "shove" and Custer did not hesitate.

60

61

The Last Stand

IT WAS NOON ON JUNE 25, 1876 WHEN GUSTER LED HIS REGIMENT TOWARD THE valley of the Little Big Horn. Close to the headwaters of Ash Creek, later to be called Reno Creek, which ran down to the river, Custer called a halt. The orders he gave to his officers and men were clear and were evidently formulated more with the intention of blocking the escape of the Indians than provoking an all out battle. They involved splitting his forces into three parts in a scaled down version of the original overall strategy of Terry's three columns. Custer had to undertake the work of Terry's and Crook's columns as well as his own.

To Benteen, Custer allocated Troops D, H and K, ordering him to feel to the left, scanning the country, sweeping the bluffs to the south and herding hostile Indians back toward the village, blocking their escape route to the south and west. To Captain McDougall went Troop B to take charge of the mule train bringing up the rear of Benteen. Major Marcus A. Reno was given command of Troops A, G and M, while Custer took the remaining Troops C, E, F, I and L. Benteen took off southward with his detachment and Reno, followed by Custer, moved down toward the valley of the Little Big Horn.

Major Reno, a graduate of West Point, had been a captain in the First Cavalry at the outbreak of the Civil War and had served with distinction, earning promotions for gallant and meritorious services in battle. He had been appointed colonel of the Twelfth Pennsylvania Volunteer Cavalry on January 1, 1865 and brevetted brigadier-general of Volunteers toward the end of the war. He had joined the Seventh Cavalry in December 1869 as a major, but had little experience of Indian fighting until the Big Horn action. His relations with Custer were always maintained on a military plane and there is no evidence of any real social contact between them, but although it has never been suggested that Reno had ever been as rabidly anti-Custer as had Benteen, a footnote in Cyrus Townsend Brady's *Indian Fights and Fighters* hints that Reno's relations with Custer had not been friendly and, in fact, were so inimical that before the last campaign Custer was begged not to entrust command of any supporting movement to Reno. But Custer never would allow personal considerations to cheat anybody of rightful command.

In the book, *The Soldiers*, David Nevin stated that Reno was court-martialled

Major Marcus Reno,
accused of cowardice for
failing to break through the
Indian ring to relieve Custer.

63

twice and that the second time, he was dismissed the service for "conduct unbecoming an officer and a gentleman." His first offence included peeping through a parlour window at the daughter of a colonel while she was chatting with her parents. He also had had an affair with the wife of a fellow officer who was away on duty. In 1880, fourteen years after the Big Horn, he was indeed found guilty by general court-martial of "conduct unbecoming" and dismissed the service, having been charged that while drunk he had become involved in a brawl in a public billiard saloon in which he assaulted another officer. Reno had always been a heavy drinker and the cloud that hung over him after the Little Big Horn may have made him more inclined than ever to reach for the bottle. Perhaps the brawl had been provoked by an offensive reference to Reno's part in the controversial battle. Whatever it was, hard drinking and a penchant for affairs with the ladies were always considered flaws in Reno's character, which had often caused him trouble and aroused some animosity toward him. But until the Battle of the Little Big Horn his bravery had never been impugned, nor it seemed had there been any reason for doing so.

The forces of Custer and Reno marched parallel to each other down the Reno Creek to a spot called Lone Tepee about eleven miles away where Reno, having reported seeing the head of an Indian village, was detailed by Custer to move off and take up a position to strike the south of the village. At about 2 a.m. Reno with his troops, and Lieutenant Varnum with most of his scouts, headed toward the valley. Later Reno stated that Custer told him he would support him.

When a general such as Custer said he would support an attack, Reno must have known full well what he meant by that. Custer did not say he would be in support of Reno which could have, indeed, implied that he would be in the rear of Reno. He said he would support Reno and that meant, without the slightest doubt, that he would attack the Indian village with Reno. Custer, when in command during any campaign, never supported from the rear.

In any case, as Reno's men cantered away down the valley they could see some distance ahead of them on their right flank, on the high bluffs across the river, Custer with a group of his officers, waving encouragingly before disappear-

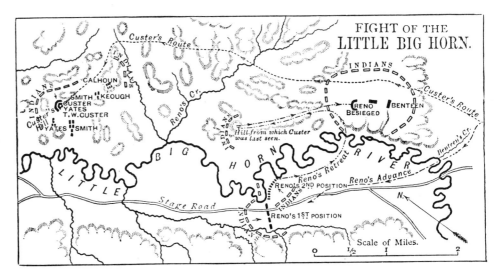

ing over the brow of a hill. There could never be any question about whether or not Custer intended to follow in the wake of Reno.

Reno headed his force to a ford to water the horses for the last time before the impending battle. Then the men crossed the ford and reformed on the other side where Reno deployed his skirmishers and advanced cautiously down the valley for a few miles. But the Indians saw them coming and came from the village to meet them, some on horseback, some on foot. The Indians appeared somewhat surprised by Reno's approach. They preferred to fight on horseback and, in order to give the other braves a chance to mount, those already on horseback galloped around frenziedly to raise a swirling dust screen. At first the Indians seemed more inclined to fall back than stand and fight but, as more Indians mounted up, they rallied. Reno realised that he had not caught the Indians completely napping even if they had acted surprised at first, and that he was face to face with a formidable force. He hesitated and decided to retreat even before he became in active contact with the Indians. Perhaps he should have pressed home his attack but it is evident, knowing full well that Custer was not behind him, he made no effort to cut through into the enemy which heavily outnumbered his own force of about one-hundred-and-sixty, ignoring what else Custer might be doing at the time. Reno's timidity had lost him the initiative.

Reno ordered his men to halt and dismount and while a skirmish line of eighty men was left to cover them, the rest retired, leading their horses into a timbered area not far away. Yet most of the Indians were still hundreds of yards distant. But soon the Indian pressure began to build up and Reno's left flank was turned. The troopers found themselves caught in a deadly crossfire and began to cluster together, hampering their own fire. The Arikara scouts on the left flank broke and fled precipitately, not stopping, it was said, until they were back on the Powder River. The Sioux also moved men up river to Reno's right flank, to the woods where troopers were nervously waiting with their horses.

Reno ordered the skirmishers to fall back to the woods to join the others, as they were beginning to yield to pressure. In the woods and thick undergrowth, instead of remounting for an immediate counter-attack, they waited and the Indians were able to come in close and set fire to the dry river-bottom grass and buffalo-berry brush. Then as the fire spread into the undergrowth, catching the cottonwoods and elders, braves crawled in closer still under cover of the acrid smoke, shooting into the bewildered troops and their terrified horses. Flames crackled all around the floundering soldiers, flying sparks stung their hands and cheeks, bullets ricocheted off the trees and showers of arrows swished through the foliage. The shrill war whoops of the Indians, the whinnying and stomping of the frenzied horses, added to the confusion. Yet, despite the hectic action, Reno's casualties had been few. However, to Reno and the men on the spot their position must have seemed untenable, and Reno ordered a retreat to the bluffs on the far side of the river.

In the pandemonium some of the soldiers did not hear the orders, but when they noticed their comrades mounting they stopped firing to join them. During

Plan of the campaign area of the Little Big Horn, showing the progress of Custer and Reno after they separated.

65

Big Chief Sitting Bull, famous
Sioux medicine man, as he
appeared in 1881.

66

Chief Two Moon of the
Northern Cheyennes, allies
of the Sioux at the Little Big
Horn.

67

a lull in the fighting a party of Sioux had dashed into the woods to a clearing where Reno was standing discussing the confused situation with Bloody Knife. A Sioux bullet shattered Bloody Knife's skull, splattering the face of the harrassed Reno with blood, fragments of bone and bits of brain. The suddenness and the impact of the horrible experience must have shaken Reno, which is not surprising. He reacted uncertainly. He ordered the men who had already mounted to dismount, but then, realising that his original plan was to retreat, ordered them back into the saddle again. In the situation of near panic and with the utmost difficulty in relaying orders to the scattered troops, the remounting of the men took place in a most desultory fashion. Eventually they were ready to leave and started to break out of the wood in a disorderly column of fours, under a withering crossfire, toward the ford where earlier they had entered the valley. Reno led his men in what he claimed to have been a charge, which it was of a sort, as the retreating force, beset on all sides by a relentless enemy sensing victory, had to force a breakthrough.

Several wounded had to be left behind, but because of the deteriorating circumstances of Reno's position and the necessity for a desperate dash to the ford, the only alternative to leaving the wounded was to shoot them. As the troopers made the frantic dash from the woods there could be no rearguard. The Indians were not pressing the retreating force through the woods but were appearing on their flanks, galloping parallel to the river, shooting at the fleeing troopers as though they were buffalo in a hunt. Fortunately for the disorganised soldiers, in the wild melee the Indian marksmanship was poor, but the Indian pressure did force the fugitives to the left, away from the ford and into the river.

Chief Gall, seeing Reno retreating to the river, rode off with a band of warriors to sweep across the river further down and cut him off. Luckily for the hard-pressed troopers, they found a pony trail to where there was a five-foot drop to another ford, but they were forced to a narrow pocket on the other side which was surrounded by bluffs, some of them up to eighty-foot high. Cavalrymen had to struggle up the steep, crumbling sides with their exhausted horses as Indians closed in on the milling troopers below, pulling them from their mounts and clubbing them with their tomahawks. Horses toppled back on their riders, crushing them or throwing them to be pounced upon by knife-wielding savages, while along the bluffs, Indians from downstream fired at the soldiers emerging from the water.

Some of the troopers had kept up a running fight as they fled from the woods. Dr De Wolf had reigned in his horse the better to fire back at his pursuers and was killed, as was Lieutenant McIntosh when he tried to rally his men. At the river bank, Lieutenant Hodgson was hit in the leg and his horse was shot from beneath him. Sergeant Criswell went to rescue him but Hodgson was hit again and killed. Criswell then returned to recover the body and bring back abandoned saddlebags laden with sorely needed ammunition. For his bravery the sergeant was awarded the Medal of Honour. Charley Reynolds, brought down on his way to the crossing, fought to a finish from behind the body of his dead horse. There was no lack of bravery on the part of the out-manoeuvred cavalrymen that day.

The survivors of Reno's force eventually gathered on the top of the bluffs, having lost a third of their numbers. Lieutenant De Rudio and fifteen men were missing but arrived on the bluff safely the next day. Meanwhile Reno prepared to meet another attack. Although the sound of firing was still heard, it seemed to be coming from somewhere near the direction of the centre of the Indian village. Half an hour later, during a brief respite, Reno saw the approach of Benteen's column.

Benteen had marched off with his detachment to probe to the left, moving from bluff to bluff. The point of his departure had been fifteen miles from the place where the bodies of Custer and his men would be found three days later. Benteen had encountered few signs of Indians and there had been little water in the rough, inhospitable country through which he had led his weary force. He had finally turned toward the valley of the Little Big Horn, just ahead of McDougall and the supply train. Benteen was riding ahead of his troops when Trumpeter Martini rode up to him with a message from Custer, addressed to Benteen and signed by Cook, Custer's adjutant. It was roughly scrawled, short and simple. It read, "Benteen. Come on Big Village. Be quick. Bring Packs. P.S.: Bring pacs."

It was obvious that the order was urgent. The P.S. repeating the request for packs showed how urgent, and the fact that the "k" had been left out of "packs" showed the haste in which the message had been written.

The packs referred to in the message contained ammunition and Benteen could have been in no doubt about Custer's need. Martini claimed that he had seen Reno in action as he rode past, coming from Custer and on to find Benteen, but stated that Benteen had given him no chance to tell him about it. Martini, who was Italian, spoke indifferent English at that time and Benteen was impatient. Later Martini claimed that the testimony he gave at the court of inquiry had been made by the court to show that he had been told to pass on the message to Captain McDougall in charge of the pack guard, but Martini denied that he so had been instructed by Benteen, nor had Benteen asked him to pass on the message to Lieutenant Mathey, the officer in charge of the packs, although the mule train was only a mile behind. Captain Weir had come up and Benteen handed him the message and had sent Martini to join one of the troops of cavalry.

Benteen chose to disobey Custer's order. He claimed that Martini had indicated that Custer had pressed the Indians to retreat and Benteen did not see any reason why time should be wasted bothering about the packs.

Perhaps he wanted to make sure to be in at the kill when Custer fell upon the retreating Indians. Benteen continued the march and soon firing was heard from the valley. Benteen's first sight of fighting was of a dozen or so dismounted men on the river bottom, surrounded by eight or nine hundred Indians. Benteen saw fit then to branch off to the left and soon came upon the rest of Reno's men

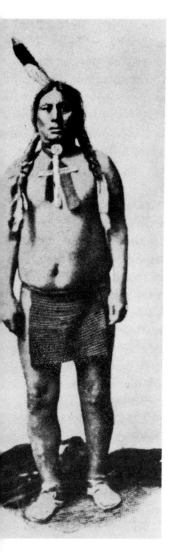

Photograph by D. F. Barry of Chief Gall, who was a little leaner at the time of the battle of the Little Big Horn.

69

Map of the battlefield from the *New York Herald*, November 16, 1877.

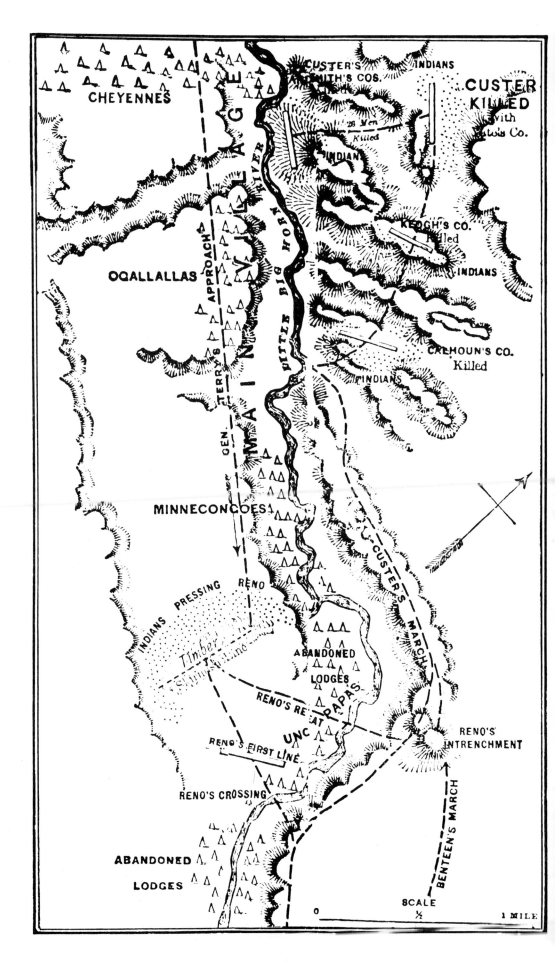

Map of the battlefield drawn
by Russell White Bear,
general secretary of the Crows.

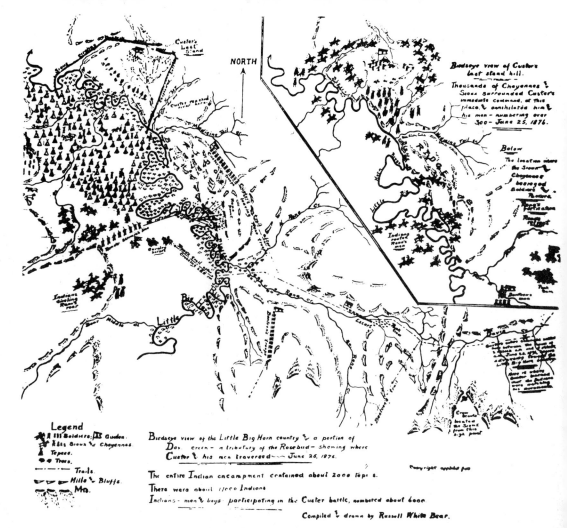

NORTH

Birdseye view of Custers
last stand hill.

Thousands of Cheyennes &
Sioux surrounded Custers
immediate command, at this
place, & annihilated him &
his men - numbering over
300 - June 25, 1876.

Below

The location where
the Sioux &
Cheyennes
besieged
Reno.

Legend

Birdseye view of the Little Big Horn country & a portion of
Da_ creek - a tributary of the Rosebud - showing where
Custer & his men traversed - June 25, 1876.

The entire Indian encampment contained about 2000 tepees.

There were about 11,000 Indians

Indians - men & boys participating in the Custer battle, numbered about 6000.

Compiled & drawn by Russell White Bear.

Lieutenant Maguire's map of
the battlefield, September
1876.

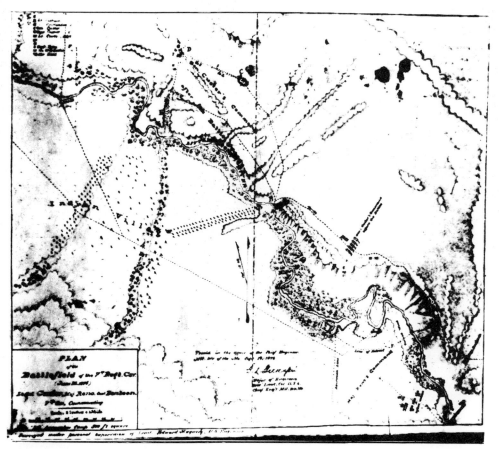

71

at bay. Reno had seen Benteen's approach and rode toward him.

Benteen asked Reno about Custer's whereabouts and showed him Custer's last order. Reno replied that he did not know where Custer was and told Benteen what had transpired since he had last seen him and how he would have imagined Custer to be close at hand when the battle had started. Reno was agitated and excited and was undecided about what his own next move should be. Custer's

Lieutenant W. W. Cook, Custer's adjutant, who signed the ''packs'' message.

Indian Raider
by Alan Willow.

Custer's Last Stand
by D. McLoughlin, 1949

Short Bull, Sioux.

message to Benteen had been explicit. It had asked him to "come quick." Martini had indicated Custer's position, which was somewhere ahead of Reno. Having been joined by Benteen and made cognisant of the situation regarding Custer, it was up to Reno to order a combined effort to get through to him. They knew that, by then, Custer must be heavily engaged, yet they hung back, Benteen making no effort to influence his weary superior. Reno said he wanted to wait for the supply train as he was in need of ammunition. Benteen's men were ordered to share their ammunition with Reno's troopers but still Reno made no move. With Indians still in the vicinity it was a difficult decision for Reno, and Benteen was content to leave it to him, although his orders from Custer had been clear enough.

A line of skirmishers was thrown out around the bluffs and a water party tried to move down to the river to bring back water which was desperately needed by the beleaguered troopers. The river was enfiladed by sporadic fire from some Indians on the banks, but the main Indian force had withdrawn. Prolonged firing could be heard coming from the north and to both Reno and Benteen it must have been patent that Custer was deeply committed in battle.

It was time for a concerted effort by Reno. The combined forces of Reno and Benteen added up to three hundred men, half of whom – Benteen's men – had not yet been in action, and officers and men wondered why Reno was hesitating. Had the earlier mauling at the hands of the Indians made him more cautious than ever? Did the idea of cocky Custer out on a limb with the prospect of having to beat a hasty retreat give Benteen some satisfaction?

With the sound of small-arms fire growing heavier some of the officers were becoming more uneasy about the danger to Custer and begged Reno to be allowed to break through to him. Finally, Captain Thomas Weir of D Troop, an admirer of Custer, having cleared his path of Indians, decided to make a move. Without orders from Reno or Benteen he set off downstream with his men toward the sound of the firing. Lieutenant Edgerly, Weir's second-in-command, chose to assume that Reno had given orders to advance and led his own group forward along the ravine below the bluff along which Weir was moving. Then, at a signal from his superior, he joined him on the bluffs. So the men advanced on their own initiative to the point where Custer had last been seen. The view from there was over ridges and valleys and beyond, and a few miles away they could see hordes of mounted Indians and could hear heavy firing. However, it was clear to the loyal officers that whatever was befalling Custer they, on their own, were powerless to intervene.

McDougall had eventually arrived, unmolested, with the pack train at about 4.30 p.m., not very long after Benteen had joined Reno on the bluffs. Benteen went to investigate Weir's advance and, seeing him returning, threw out a defensive line to allow his saddened troop through. At about five o'clock Reno finally decided to make a move and marched along the ridge to the point reached by Weir and Edgerly, arriving there at 5.30 p.m. But now it was too late; hordes of exulting Indians, fresh from victory over Custer, came surging toward them in clouds of alkaline dust and once again Reno thought it prudent to retreat to take up defensive positions and try to keep the enemy at bay, leaving Custer to fend for himself.

Once again an officer chose to act without orders. Lieutenant Godfrey and his junior officer, Lieutenant Hare of the rearguard K Troop, dismounted their men and deployed them to cover the retreat. They managed to hold off the Indians until the retirement was complete and then successfully rejoined their comrades. It was as well that Godfrey had not waited for orders. His initiative saved the command from a dangerous situation. The retirement was back to their previous position on the bluffs and the men were posted around the ridge across the depression on a hill to the right to cover the packs and a field hospital that had been set up, covering all sides except the river side where an attack was hardly feasible because of the height of the bluffs and the distance involved. On the right, on top of the bare break of the ridge, Benteen's H Troop, without adequate cover, was commanded by higher ridges. The hospital and packs were defended by Moylan's troopers who actually used the packs for cover as the Indians started to close and pour in a heavy fire. The soldiers, flat on their stomachs or kneeling in depressions, returned the fire steadily.

The Indians began their attack by pressing hard against Reno's left flank, but gradually worked around the position until fighting raged all along the line. It continued for three hours before it began to ease off in the failing light and ceased, except for occasional shots, at about nine at night. Under cover of darkness the troopers were able to move about and consolidate their positions by digging weapon pits, using whatever tools they could improvise.

The night was far from peaceful, however. From the village came the noise of the triumphant Indians, celebrating their victories with chanting, whooping and yelling, as well as the awful beat of monotonous drumming and shooting. Huge bonfires could be seen blazing in the village, casting long shadows of Indian dancers as they shuffled round the flaring flames, with eddies of smoke pinkly reflected above the tepees.

The tired battle-weary soldiers up on the bluffs shivered, wondering with dread whether the Indians had captured any prisoners and were putting them to torture and the stake. To remind the troopers that they had not been forgotten, at two in the morning Indians up on the hills fired at them from out of the darkness, but they did not attack. At first light the Indians prepared to resume the battle and began pressing nearer and nearer the beleaguered positions on the bluffs. Benteen's exposed position came in for heavy punishment and many of his men were wounded as the morning wore on. Benteen realised that his position could soon become untenable and his exhausted men, short of ammunition, might be forced back or overrun.

Benteen ordered Lieutenant Gibson to hang on at all costs while he hurried off to Reno to request reinforcements. He had difficulty in persuading Reno to grant his request and Gibson sent a runner asking Benteen to hurry as his situation was becoming desperate. Reno finally agreed to send Captain French

74

with M Troop but, on the way back to his position, Benteen could see that the Indians were pressing even harder against the straining defences and bold action was needed to break up the enemy concentration. Benteen rushed back to Reno and urged him to order an attack to break the vice closing about them. Again it took a good deal of persuasion but Reno finally assented and told Benteen to prepare the men and give the signal to charge. Benteen raced back to his position, formed up his men and led them into the attack shouting, "All ready now, men. Now's your time. Give them hell! Hip! Hip! Here we go!"

The men, straining their cramped limbs, surged forward, yelling and firing their carbines. A large group of Indians had been assembling at the foot of the hill on the north side ready to charge and as the dismounted troops bore down on them, shouting and swearing, with carbines blazing, the Indians broke. Reno, encouraged by the initial success, led his men into action on the other side of the hill, forcing the Indians there to yield ground. Then Reno ordered the men back to their positions.

The sortie had broken up the immediate Indian threat but the troops' need for water was desperate. Their throats were parched and dry from excitement, heat and smoke. The men had tried sucking pebbles, chewing bread and grass roots but only water could assuage their raging thirsts. At eleven in the morning, when the fire from the Indians seemed to have slackened a little, volunteers were called for to get water. Nineteen men came forward and four of them, the best marksmen of H Troop, were detailed to give the rest covering fire from an extreme position on the brim of the bluffs overlooking the river.

The fifteen men, dangling canteens and camp kettles, crawled through undergrowth and along shallow crevices toward open space along the river bank. Then, as the four marksmen forced the Indians to keep down with rapid fire from well chosen vantage points, the troopers made a dash for the river. All the same the water party came under heavy fire, but the troopers succeeded in filling their vessels, although a few men were wounded and some of the vessels peppered. The wounded men were dragged to safety and the water taken back helped to relieve the thirsty men waiting on the bluffs. All nineteen men were decorated with Medals of Honour.

At one o'clock there seemed to be few Indians firing into the army positions, although they were still guarding the river. At two o'clock the Indian fire increased, forcing the defenders who had relaxed a little to take cover again. But by three o'clock all firing ceased and for a while there was a strange silence. Later in the afternoon the defenders saw a few horsemen below them and the grass was set alight to cause a smokescreen. At seven o'clock, emerging through the haze of smoke, a mass exodus of Indians was seen in the direction of the mountains of the Big Horn. In clouds of dust, flanked by Indian warriors, whole families were moving with all their possessions, evacuating their large village on the Little Big Horn. The defenders on the bluff were not sure whether the move was part of a ruse or a clearing of decks for further action, but they were thankful for the respite. A bold commander might have seized the opportunity to swoop down and harry the retreating Indians.

In the hours of action on the hill under assault of allegedly thousands of Indians, the desperate defence, the sorties and the water parties, only eighteen troopers were killed and fifty-two wounded. The troopers occupied a good defensive position. They had all the packs with the ammunition Custer needed. Reno's and Benteen's forces together were far greater than Custer's. Furthermore, it would seem that in actual fact the Indians ranged against them were just a holding force while the main bodies of Indians were concentrated in the attack against Custer. Reno and Benteen knew that help from Terry was on the way and was not likely to be long delayed; they knew that the rate of their casualties was such that they could hang on to their positions until Terry arrived. As far as they were concerned, Custer could take care of himself. They were all right, Jack.

Nobody can ever know what happened at the battle of the Little Big Horn. If there were any survivors of Custer's force who actually took part in that last battle, any who had managed to slip away while the fighting was yet in progress or after the last shot had been fired, none ever came forward to make such a

The Fight of the Little Big Horn; illustration from *Battles of the Nineteenth Century*, 1898.

Crow scout Curley, pictured some time after the battle.

claim except for a Crow scout called Curley. Curley's story, however, seemed to be a product of misquotations, half truths and gradual build-up with embellishments from material culled from subsequent accounts of Terry's operations.

There were, of course, the Indian warriors who had fought Custer and were present when his force was annihilated, but the various accounts taken from the Indians, most of whom spoke little English or none at all, and who were apt, as soldiers in any battle, to know only just what went on in their own immediate vicinity, who were prone to exaggeration and boasting and were, more than likely, reluctant to confess to white interlocutors exactly what part they had taken in the final onslaught, could only produce a hazy and sketchy picture. Their stories were contradictory and stories told in their own language lost a good deal in translation.

Trumpeter Martini, sent by Custer to Benteen with the famous "packs" message, gave a detailed account of his part in the expedition, but he could not, of course, give any account of what went on after he finally rode out of sight of his comrades. All the same, his full story as told to Colonel W. A. Graham was

Rain-in-the-Face, Sioux chief in war regalia, and (far right) Low Dog, Ogallala, chief of the Sioux.

77

years after the battle, when he was old and feeble, when his English was better but perhaps not his memory, when situations seemed simpler in retrospect, doubts had been resolved and certain unpleasant thoughts buried, when protracted publicity had extricated the essence and added embellishment and invention.

At the time of the Big Horn, Martini was a green Italian who spoke and understood English imperfectly, which is probably why Lieutenant Cook wrote out the message for him after Custer had galloped up and given it to him verbally. That message was too important and urgent to commit just to the trumpeter's memory. Martini, no matter what reservations there might be about accepting his story in toto, was the last man left after the Little Big Horn to have seen Custer alive. It is therefore worthwhile to read his account in full and it is published in the appendix.

Below Captain Thomas Custer. *Foot of the page* forage master Boston Custer.

When Custer had looked down at Reno and waved his hat before going off on his final journey, he had a view of the Indian village over several miles and, when he had continued on to another vantage point and saw the vast extent of the village, he resolved to skirt it and come in nearer to the rear of it. He must have reasoned that by the time he and Reno hit the village and fought their way through to each other, Benteen's troops would be needed to join in the fight or the chase of the fleeing Indians, and the packs of ammunition would be vital in either case. It was then that Custer had sent Martini off with the message to Benteen. The last Martini had seen of Custer was as he led his force down Medicine Trail Coulee toward a ford.

At three o'clock, Reno had already run into trouble and been forced back. Chief Gall, moving his band of Indians across the river to outflank Reno, must have sighted Custer moving over to cross the river in the opposite direction. Gall knew Reno was tied down and had already gauged that Reno, having reacted the way he had done when he had first encountered the Indians outside the village and then suffered a severe reverse, would be in no mood to attack his flank or rear, even were pressure taken off him. Gall immediately sent word of the situation to Chief Crazy Horse who was pressing Reno hard. Reno could be dealt with later. Leaving enough warriors to keep the shaken troopers down under their hats, Crazy Horse and his braves, joined by other Indians who had not yet been engaged, galloped off through the village to swing round Custer as he was being headed off the river by Gall.

Perhaps Custer joined battle with Gall immediately but, surprised by the huge number of warriors, made for the high open ground to the north the better to deploy for a charge, as any experienced cavalry commander would have done under similar circumstances. What Custer had not known was that the redoubtable Crazy Horse had been in the Indian village and, at the head of hundreds of his warriors, was sweeping through the camp seeking to head him off, turn him and outflank him.

With two formidable forces of yelling Indians converging on him, Custer realised that his advance on the village had been blocked and that he would now

78

Top of the page Lieutenant James Calhoun, Custer's brother-in-law, and (above) Henry Armstrong Reed, Custer's nephew.

have to fight a defensive battle. However, he had already sent a message to Benteen to hurry and with what looked like the bulk of any conceivable Indian force around him, Reno to the south would be able to push up through the village and relieve the pressure on Custer, giving him the opportunity to rally a charge. It was not working exactly the way he had planned, but it was a situation with which he would have thought he could cope. In any case, Gibbon and Terry could be expected to arrive the next day and, if he just held the Indians at bay until then, he would have achieved the purpose of the whole expedition.

The deployment of Custer's troops on the Little Big Horn could be assumed by the position of the bodies on the battlefield after the Indians had gone and Terry surveyed the gruesome and melancholy scene. It seemed that Custer's troopers had been dismounted to occupy the ridges, with the horses placed in the rear. L Troop, commanded by Lieutenant Calhoun, Custer's brother-in-law, had been positioned on the left. Next came I Troop, commanded by Captain Miles Keogh, then the companies commanded by Algernon E. Smith, E Troop, and George W. Yates with F Troop. On the extreme right, under Custer's brother Tom, was C Troop.

As the Indian attackers rode back and forth across the front of the troopers, firing with long range rifles far superior to the soldiers' carbines, the soldiers had fallen back steadily. Custer, with the three troops on the right, occupied higher ground, but Crazy Horse's warriors swarmed up the hill behind Custer and, topping the rise, came roaring down on him. Fighting fiercely, the troopers had driven them off, but as the afternoon wore on ammunition must have been running low. The troopers' horses had been stampeded, taking with them the reserve supply of ammunition.

Many of Gall's braves dismounted, crawled close to the position of L Troop and began picking off the troopers, using bows and arrows. Then, as the almost helpless soldiers tried to close ranks, Indians rose shrieking to their feet to let loose a final flurry of arrows and shots, and mounted warriors raced in among the demoralised men with knife, tomahawk and lance and despatched the survivors who fought back with clubbed rifle, pistol and bare hands until they finally succumbed.

I Troop suffered a similar fate, with the soldiers going down in last desperate hand-to-hand struggles, as smoke and dust swirled around them and the ghastly sight of wild-eyed, painted savages chilled the blood in their veins before they died.

Higher up the ridges Custer drew up his men to make a final stand. The situation was past hope but there could be no going up. Custer's men occupied a relatively strong defensive position but their ammunition was fast running out and their carbines were fouling. When the weapons became overheated, the soft copper bullets expanded, jamming the barrels, or the ejectors cut through the cartridge rims jamming the breaches. Sometimes a trooper under fire and enormous pressure was still able to prise loose a jammed cartridge and fire one or two more rounds before his weapon jammed again.

Custer's group was forced in closer and closer until they were huddled, fighting almost back to back. Men resorted to pistols and used their carbines as clubs. They crouched at bay, eyes wild and smarting with smoke, bodies wet and prickly with sweat, and their hearts almost bursting with fear as they faced the inevitable. Only madness snapping the mind could anaesthetise the horror of the final descending tomahawk or war club and the slashing knife. Arrows fell about the troopers, finding fleshy targets. Crudely made Indian bullets spurted up dust or tore into bone and flesh.

Gall and Crazy Horse finally massed on the flanks and attacked as Crow King and Rain-in-the-Face led a frontal assault. Custer's position was overrun and in the ensuing bloody hand-to-hand struggle every surviving man on the hill was savagely stabbed and hacked to death. A group of thirty troopers had tried to reach the river and were cut down in their tracks. A few isolated bodies were found of men who had attempted to make a run for it or to get through the lines with a message for help. In less than one hour Custer and his men, all two-hundred-and-thirty of them, had been slain and the victors, laughing and chattering excitedly, moved about the stark battlefield, stripping the dead, scalping, hacking, mutilating, decapitating, leaving the ghastly pale remains in pools of dried blood for horrified but luckier soldiers to find.

Terry and Gibbon, having relieved Reno who was in no danger by the time they arrived, found General Custer on the battlefield where he had fallen surrounded by his men. He was stripped naked and had been shot in the side and in the head, but had not been scalped or otherwise mutilated. With him at the Little Big Horn had died those he most loved and trusted. They included his brother Tom, who had won two Congressional Medals of Honour in the Civil War; Calhoun, Custer's brother-in-law; Boston Custer, another of the general's brothers, and Autie Reed, Custer's nephew.

Stalwart officers killed in the battle were young Lieutenant Crittenden who had volunteered to accompany Custer; Smith, the commander of E Troop and battered hero of the storming of Fort Fisher; Keogh, the oldest soldier of I Troop, veteran Yates and young Sturgis. Also killed were newspaper correspondent Mark Kellog and scout Charley Reynolds. Some bodies were not recovered. Doctor Lord, Lieutenant Sturgis, Porter and Harrington were missing, but it was never doubted that they had been killed, either near the field of battle or as prisoners. Nobody ever found out, but later clothes of Sturgis and Porter were discovered on the abandoned site of the Indian village.

So Custer was dead. He had died in combat. Even his bitterest enemies could not deny that, whatever they did to revile him, to belittle his military exploits, to crticise his character and make him the scapegoat for Terry's and Crook's failures, although he had been the only commander who had actually seized the initiative in the campaign. Perhaps Custer's defeat had been inevitable when he split his forces; not because the division had been a bad move, but because of the characters of the men who commanded the other two groups. It was some-

roadside published on July
, 1876, announcing death of
uster. Despite his fame the
pesetters could not spell his
ame.

GREAT BATTLE WITH THE INDIANS.

Terrific Slaughter

GEN. CUSTAR'S COMMAND ANNIHILATED.

CUSTAR KILLED!

Three Hundred Dead Left on the Field.

Gen. Custar's Two Brothers, a Nephew, Brother-in-Law, and 17 Commissioned Officers Among the Killed.

Special Dispatch to The San Diego Union

STILLWATER, Montana Ter., July 2.—
Mug. Taylor, scout for General Gibbons, arrived here last night direct
from Little Horn river. He brings
intelligence that General Custar found
an Indian camp, of about two thousand lodges. on the Little Horn, and
immediately attacked it. He took five
companies, and charged into the thickest portion of the camp. Nothing is
known of the operations of this detachment, only as they are traced by
the dead. Major Reno commanded
seven other companies, and attacked
the lower portion of the camp.

The Indians poured in a murderous
fire from all directions, and the greatest
portion fought on horse-back.

General Custar, his two brothers,
nephew and brother-in-law were all
killed, and not one of his detachment

escaped. Two hundred and seven men
were buried in one place, and the number of killed is estimated at three hundred, with only thirty-one wounded.

The Indians surrounded Major
Reno's command, and held them for
one day in the hills, cut off from water,
until General Gibbons' command came
in sight, when they broke camp in the
night and left.

The Seventh company fought like
tigers, but were overcome by brute
force. The Indian loss cannot be estimated, as they bore off and *cached* the
most of their killed. The remnant of
the Seventh Cavalry, together with
General Gibbons' command are returning to the mouth of the Little Horn,
where a steamer lies, The Indians got
all the arms of the killed soldiers.

There were seventeen commissioned
officers killed. The whole of the Custar family died at the head of their
column. The exact loss was not known.
Both the adjutant and sergeant major
were killed.

The Indian camp was from three to
five miles long, and was twenty miles
up the Little Horn from its mouth.
The Indians actually pulled men from
their horses in some instances.

The above is confirmed by other letters, which say that Custar met a fearful disaster.

The Boyeman (Montana) *Times*, Ex-
tra, confirms the report, and says the
whole number killed was three hundred and fifteen. Gen. Gibbons joined
the command at Reno. When the Indians left the battle field looked like a
slaughter-pen, as it really was, being
in a narrow ravine. The dead were
horribly mutilated. The situation now
looks serious.

General Terry arrived at Gibbons'
camp on a steamer, and crossed his
command over to join General Custar,
who knew it was coming before the fight
occurred. Lieut. Crittenden, son of
Gen. Crittenden, was also among the
killed.

Custer in characteristic pose.

thing about which Custer might possibly have been more prudent. He knew Benteen and Reno well enough not to have put so much faith in them.

The argument whether or not Custer disobeyed Terry's orders makes no difference to the facts. A fact is that Custer attacked the largest force of Indians ever assembled for battle, whether he knew it at the time or not. A fact is that he paid with his life for his own mistakes and the mistakes and failures of others. A fact is that after the Little Big Horn the Plains Indians were finished as a fighting force forever.

82

Post mortems

IN THE EDITORIAL COLUMN OF THE *Chicago Tribune* PUBLISHED ON JULY 7, 1876, ten days after Terry had reached the battlefield of the Little Big Horn, this was written of General Custer, "Custer . . . was a brave, brilliant soldier, handsome and dashing, but he was reckless, hasty and impulsive, preferring to make a daredevil rush and take risks rather than to move slower and with more certainty, and it was his own madcap haste, rashness and love of fame that cost him his own life, and cost the service the loss of many brave officers and gallant men. . . He preferred to make a reckless dash and take the consequences in the hope of making a personal victory and adding to the glory of another charge, rather than wait for a sufficiently powerful force to make the fight successful and share the glory with the others. He took the risk and he lost."

This was instant evaluation and assessment before full details of the battle were known, before any investigations or inquiries, and the tone of the editorial was to set the pattern for the Custer controversy that was to rage thereafter. Every facet of Custer's character and his actions would be defined and argued, confirmed or denied, and when all else had been analysed, criticised, praised or vilified, even his looks would be dragged into the arena. In a letter to Goldin on August 23, 1894, Benteen wrote, "I am somewhat inclined to think the committee in charge of preparation of sketches for "Squiers" 7th. Cav. book is somewhat on the close corporation biz., but the hot-shot I throw in protesting against Custer's ugly phiz being shown in the front of the book is having its effect, and I think the volume will come out without any frontispiece in the shape of a portrait."

It was rather like a small boy having run out of argument, resorting to personal remarks and name-calling. This was mere pettiness, but of course Custer's dashing appearance was all part of the legend and Custer, quite consciously, did much to foster it, in much the same way as celebrities of today. The studied carelessness of his dress and flamboyant design of his uniform, the buckskins, white broad-brimmed hats, crimson neckerchiefs and high boots all helped to draw attention to himself as did his long hair. But his locks were yellow, his eyes brilliant blue, his complexion florid. He had courage, ability and stamina and, like so many gifted people, cashed in on his assets. As far as the press was concerned Custer was good copy, of course, as is any such outstanding figure in any

Newspaper illustration of the Reno court of inquiry, held at Chicago in 1879.

walk of life. Custer attracted not only praise, admiration and flattery, but also criticism, rumours of scandal, jealousy and hatred. With his panache, literary ability, public appeal and courage in battle, he was too much like an ideal hero of fiction for cynics, disgruntled veterans of the Civil War and crooked politicians to stomach.

Custer was said to be reckless, irresponsible, impetuous, imprudent and vainglorious and after the Battle of the Little Big Horn, when he was no longer present to defend himself, his enemies and their fellow travellers had a field day. The Indians did not scalp or mutilate Custer after death but what they failed to do Custer's enemies tried to do. His friends and admirers rose in his defence, and partisans of both factions rushed to join in the fray. Officers and men, Indian scouts, Indians formerly hostile who had taken part in the Little Big Horn, including the great Indian chief and medicine man of the Sioux nation, Big Chief Sitting Bull, who had masterminded the huge concentration of Indians, all stepped into the arena. They all added to the welter of evidence, speculation, embellishment and invention, but the only piece of physical evidence, other than the mute corpses on the battlefield after the Little Big Horn, was Custer's last message written by his adjutant, W. Cook, calling for Benteen and the packs.

In a letter to his wife, written on July 4, 1876 from the camp of the Seventh Cavalry on the Yellowstone River, Benteen mentions the "packs" message which he still had in his possession. He said the message, brought to him by Trumpeter Martini of his own company, saved his life. In this long letter Benteen lost no time. He blamed Custer for the defeat on the Little Big Horn, arbitrarily attributing it to his glory seeking. Benteen's version of incidents during the campaign varies a good deal from versions given by other participants in the series of events and, in fact, from subsequent versions of his own. He also wrote

84

disparagingly of other officers.

As it was from Benteen that so much ammunition to attack Custer's record and image, was drawn, a study of this letter written soon after Custer's death and a letter written years later, to Goldin on November 10, 1891, reveals the style of Benteen's character assassinations with the sneers and innuendos, his treatment of facts and his self praise and righteousness. In the letter to his wife, Benteen wrote that Weir's company had been sent to communicate with Custer when in truth Weir, in frustration, had taken his troop without orders to an observation point from where he hoped he would be able to see signs of Custer and to help him if possible. In the Goldin letter, after it had been assessed during the preceding years that Weir's action had been a futile gesture, Benteen sneers that Weir sallied out without orders. Both these letters, except for material deleted as irrelevant, appear in the appendix.

The bodies on the battlefield of the Big Horn had not yet been buried before the war of words started, and it was natural that the battles would rage fiercest around Custer, Benteen and Reno. Still the war goes on. The two surviving commanders of Custer's column, Benteen and Reno, were able to counter any attack made on them. They had the benefit of hindsight and collusion, of being able to collaborate when it suited their purpose to defend the parts they had played in the campaign, and they could draw on partisan corroboration. Benteen, who openly despised Custer, and Reno who had no love for Custer and was forced to be very much on the defensive for his part in the campaign, had most of the advantages in the post mortems after the battle.

Whittaker wrote a letter to Congress that was published in July 1876, accusing Major Marcus Reno of gross cowardice during the campaign, and Reno was compelled to ask for an army court of inquiry. A court was convened in Chicago on January 13, 1879, and the hearing lasted for over three weeks. After a mass of testimony that filled 1,300 pages the court exonerated Reno. This did not satisfy his critics. They were unconvinced and accused the Army of covering up.

Reno had been accused of cowardice. He probably knew fear at times, as do all soldiers, but whatever happened on the Big Horn, Reno was no coward and his record in the Civil War was there to prove it. When he led his force toward the Indian village and had run into a large mass of hostile Indians, perhaps he thought that his force being small, the best thing to do was to move back, drawing the Indians on, and give Custer a better chance to charge into the attack from the rear. Perhaps the situation got out of hand in the heat of hectic, disjointed action and for a while he did lose his head. All the same, Reno did manage to extricate his men from a tangled situation, withdraw to a good defensive position, and hold out until Benteen arrived on the scene. He showed no cowardice in the way he fought and had done his best to resolve the invidious position he had got himself into. Perhaps he did think Custer would help retrieve the situation.

It was suggested that Reno was drunk during the action. That was hardly likely. If he had been drinking to excess, the effect of the fierce Indian attacks would have soon sobered him. If, indeed, his judgment had been affected it was not because of drinking. During World War I, before going "over the top", British infantrymen were issued with a rum ration to help them face the terrifying ordeal ahead. Reno was suddenly confronted by a dilemma and had to make a quick decision. He played his cards as he saw them and he could have been wrong. But perhaps not from where he was sitting.

Benteen rode in to join Reno, without being molested by the Indians, not long after Reno had been chased across the river. William E. Morris, who had been a private in M Troop under Captain Thomas H. French and had been wounded, later wrote about Benteen's arrival on the scene. He said, "Benteen arriving about an hour later, came up as though he was going to a funeral. By this statement I do not desire to reflect in any way upon him; he was simply in no hurry; and Müller of his troop, who occupied an adjoining cot to mine in the hospital at Fort Abraham Lincoln, told me that they walked all the way and that they heard the heavy firing while they were watering the horses. Benteen was, unquestionably, the bravest man I ever met. He held the Indians in absolute contempt and was a walking target from the time he became engaged until the end of the fight at sundown on the 26th."

Why was Benteen in no hurry? He had received the urgent "packs" message. He himself suggested that he had not wished to waste time waiting for the mule train. Trooper Morris, never doubting Benteen's bravery, was obviously nonplussed about Benteen's lethargy. Perhaps it had crossed Benteen's mind that Custer would hold up his attack until the arrival of the packs and the longer Benteen took in reaching Custer the more time there would be for Terry to reach the scene.

Benteen's troopers had recently watered their horses, had seen no action, had suffered no casualties and were fit for battle. Here was possibly an opportunity for Reno to seize the initiative. But Reno, who had been under heavy pressure and was greatly relieved by Benteen's arrival, was incapable of making a rapid assessment of the situation and immediately go on the offensive to fight through to Custer.

Benteen, as brave a soldier as any, but an implacable enemy of Custer and resenting anything he did, would be feeling that whatever situation Custer had got himself and his detachment into he had only himself to blame, and Benteen was loath to help him pull his chestnuts out of the fire. He certainly did not encourage Reno to look for Custer. He disobeyed Custer's orders about "coming quick" and the "packs." The situation was allowed to deteriorate until it was too late to do anything about Custer. Was it considered a safer bet just to sit tight and wait for Terry, leaving Custer to stew in his own juice?

Frederick William Benteen was a Virginian but in his early boyhood he moved with his family to Missouri. His father was a slave holder and a staunch secessionist. On the outbreak of the Civil War, Frederick, alone of all his family, declared for the Union and received a commission in a loyal regiment of the Missouri Cavalry. His father was furious and disowned him, but young

Benteen was undeterred. Throughout the war he served bravely and ably and, recognised by his superiors for his achievements as a competent combat leader, he earned rapid promotion. Years later he was brevetted for gallantry and leadership against hostile Indians and eventually received a well-earned brevet of brigadier-general.

He had been recommended for promotion to brigadier-general towards the end of the Civil War but after the Tenth Missouri, in which he served, had been mustered out, he was appointed colonel of a coloured regiment, a post he found distasteful. He mentions this in a letter to Goldin written October 20, 1891 and included in the appendix. He preferred to accept a subordinate commission as senior captain of the newly formed Seventh Cavalry under Custer, a man who like himself had won rapid promotion in the Civil War and had, in fact, come out of it somewhat better than had Benteen. Insight into Benteen's character is found in this letter and others of a remarkable series of letters to Goldin, a lawyer who had been a private in the Seventh Cavalry during 1876–7, and who

Benton, after his retirement from active service, was still full of hatred for the long-dead Custer.

87

contacted Benteen in 1871, starting a correspondence between them that lasted five years. The very fact of his correspondence with Goldin showed Benteen's desperate need, even twenty years after Custer's death, to find an outlet for his passionate hatred of Custer.

What had Benteen thought of his new commanding officer, a man he had never seen before joining the Seventh Cavalry at Fort Riley? Benteen reacted stiffly and resentfully at their very first meeting in Custer's private quarters. Custer proudly displayed relics, orders and books of his old cavalry division in the Cavalry Corps. Benteen wrote that Custer was trying to impress him and continued sourly that his own first impression at the interview was not a favourable one and that he himself had been on intimate terms with many great generals, none of whom had bragged in such a manner as did Custer that night. Yet Benteen was often full of self-praise and boasting. He stated that Colonel A. J. Smith, the Colonel of the Regiment, had done far greater work than Custer ever thought of and he, Benteen, had served with him. He said Smith and other officers of the post knew his record so he was not quite an "orphan or unknown," but with people who knew what he had done with a cavalry regiment and division of cavalry regiments when war was red hot.

But what was it that had really stuck in Benteen's craw? Custer had no reason to try to impress his subordinate. He knew that Benteen was as cognisant of his record as he was of Benteen's. Benteen was prejudiced and jealous of Custer even before their meeting. When he finally met his youthful commander face to face, as far as Benteen was concerned it was a case of hate at first sight and Benteen never changed his attitude, growing only more spiteful, crusty and malicious as time went on. He thought highly of himself as an officer and resented having to serve in Custer's shadow. He envied Custer his close contacts with high ranking officers, notably Sheridan, and the press.

Benteen wanted to be loved. He wanted to be loved better than Custer, whom he admitted he despised. He repeatedly and clumsily tried to show that he was, indeed, better loved. He wrote to Goldin, "I started in with my troops to make friends and soldiers of them. I would treat them like men and everybody else had to; so they got to love me." He implied that Custer did not make friends of the troops, and illustrated his own solicitude for his men. He wrote that once, on arrival at Fort Wallace, he learned that two of his men among others had been arrested for taking French leave and that the prisoners were marched through camp with heads shaved and pegged out on the plain. Benteen said that he took the affidavits of the two men to help them.

Benteen accused Custer of highhandedness and malpractice in the handling of supplies and sales of goods to his men through army post traders, but such tales savoured somewhat of the taste of a poor rebuttal to the real flavour of the damaging accusations Custer had made against the Belknap faction. He alleged that Custer was tight in his playing of cards and in money matters. Benteen rated himself highly as a poker player, as he did in so many things, boasting in his letters to Goldin about his prowess, frequently to the detriment of Custer, disparagingly referring to other players as the "Custer gang." It is evident that, in what Benteen thought was his superiority to Custer as a poker player, he found some poor consolation for his lack of skills, compared to Custer, in other fields.

An account written by Benteen to Goldin in February 1896, twenty years after Custer's death, illustrates Benteen's animosity in his curious relationship with his commander. He stated that in October 1868, immediately after Custer's sentence had been remitted and he had rejoined the regiment, Custer cast around for some officer to send to Fort Harker, Kansas, where there were three hundred horses and two hundred recruits for the Seventh Cavalry. He had been selected to go with one orderly the one-hundred-and-eighty miles through hostile territory. Benteen said that it did not daunt him a particle as he knew every mile of the district. He stated that before starting off at night, Custer had sent for him and requested that when he arrived at Harker to be kind enough to send one hundred dollars to Mrs. Custer at Fort Leavenworth, Kansas. Sneeringly, in his letter, Benteen went on to say that he had then begun to see why he had been selected. He said it was known in the regiment that he always had plenty of money. He said that the first thing he had done on reaching Harker was to send his personal cheque to Mrs. Custer.

On the way back Benteen and his recruits had gone to the rescue of a wagon train attacked by Indians and had scattered the attackers. Benteen said that all that had been in October 1869. Then he went on to say that in November 1869 Custer was to march the battalion to Fort Leavenworth where it was going for the winter and Benteen had driven his wife and child to watch the band lead the parade. While he was standing studying the horses Custer rode up to the carriage where Mrs. Benteen was sitting, shook hands with her and said goodbye, but, complained Benteen, Custer never even mentioned the one hundred dollars he still owed him. When in the winter of '69 and '70, Benteen learned from an officer from Leavenworth that Custer had made a haul at Jenison's Faro Bank, he wrote to Custer that if he had the money convenient it was high time the debt was paid, reminding him that it was ninety-one dollars, nine dollars being deductable for small amounts to square card loss adjustments. Benteen said that Custer had replied immediately to his dun, sending his cheque for ninety-two dollars which was the amount as Custer recalled it. Benteen went on to say that as one dollar would scarcely be living interest on one hundred dollars for fourteen months or over, and as he was no Shylock, lending money at an interest anyway, he coolly returned on the same day a one dollar bill thanking Custer for his promptitude in discharging the debt.

It is surprising that an officer as critical of his commander as Benteen was, should have paid out one hundred dollars for Custer in the first place. Relating such a thin story in an attempt to denigrate Custer further to Goldin was another example of Benteen's pettiness. In another letter to Goldin, Benteen harped on that loan, again attacking Custer, implying that in sending him on the one-hundred-and-eighty miles journey to Fort Harker, Custer had hoped Benteen would be killed. Yet Benteen had previously stated that Custer had purposely selected Benteen with the hundred dollars loan as the ulterior motive.

Benteen also referred to a letter to a newspaper criticising Custer's handling of the Battle of Washita, but here he hedged, alleging that the criticism was actually in a private letter he had written to a William De Gresse, a captain in his former regiment, and that it had inadvertently fallen into the hands of the newspaper. He said that when Tom Custer had pointed out the letter in the newspaper to him, Benteen had immediately recognised the letter as one he had written privately to De Gresse and had said so to Tom. But, of course, Tom had been killed at the Little Big Horn years before Benteen's neat explanations to Goldin.

Benteen wrote, "I suppose De Gresse came across a lively newspaper reporter and the letter then got to the public i.e. only the portion affecting the Washita fight. I wasn't ashamed of it; didn't care a d——n for Custer if he did owe me $100 debt of honor, and I owned straight up that I was the miscreant who had given it to the world, though I hadn't the remotest idea it would be published— the glimmer of some truth about Indian fighting.

"Well, Custer had given me a fair chance of getting scalped in sending me 180 miles alone, almost, for recruits and horses; had endeavoured to the best of his ability to get Colonel Myers and myself killed at the Washita, all of which close to death's embraces I was thoroughly aware of, and I must say wholly careless of; but the intent was perceptibly plain 'allee samee.'

"Custer paid me off for the letter in almost spot cash. Colonel William Thompson's troop was, and had been, stationed at Dodge since the birth of the regiment, and Thompson liked Dodge as a station, and he and his troop desired to remain there. I did not want it; this Custer knew. He also knew that I had had a child born and died at Harker since I left there, and that my wife was ill and came very close to death, and I am inclined to think he hadn't still forgotten that he still owed me $100 I had sent to Mrs. Custer."

Benteen lost no time in complaining behind Custer's back to Colonel Mitchell, A.D.C. and Inspector-General for General W. S. Hancock, claiming that Custer had banished him for punishment because of the newspaper letter. Benteen mentions this encounter with Mitchell in the long letter to Goldin of February 17, 1896, which is full of complaints, innuendos and unflattering remarks about the long dead Custer. Benteen referred to his visit to Custer's field, made at his own request after the battle. He wrote what he had said to a Lieutenant Maguire of Engineers after returning from the battlefield, "By the Lord Harry, old man, 'twas a ghastly sight; but what a big winner the U.S. Govt. would have been if only Custer and his gang could have been taken!"

This was a savage remark and not the sort a responsible officer normally makes to a very junior officer unless he is so carried away by hatred he is made reckless. Benteen continued to Goldin, "You know me enough to know I'd have gone through to him had it been possible to do so. At the same time, I'm only too proud to say that I despised him."

At the outbreak of the Civil War, Benteen had forsaken the cause of the

South, not because of ideological reasons – he had no love or sympathy for Negroes as he illustrated in his reaction to his being posted to a Negro regiment – but for the opportunities to further his own career. Benteen had had no compunction even about arranging the capture of his own father, a patriotic Southerner, and had not let his father know that his own son had been responsible. Yet Benteen had finished the war without the amount of recognition he wanted and thought he deserved. Disappointed and disgruntled and with a guilt feeling, Custer had become the fixation for Benteen's bitterness, turning quickly to a hatred that finally became pathological.

But was Benteen's self-confessed hatred of Custer a reason he was prepared to sacrifice him and his men rather than risk his own life and the lives of his own men, carrying out Custer's last orders in a dangerous attempt to save him? Or was Benteen's attitude rationalised pragmatism in view of what he knew of the circumstances of the campaign? One thing is certain, however. Cowardice could not have been a reason for Benteen's holding back. Benteen was no coward in battle. Custer had always known this so well that he made allowances for Benteen, ignoring his insolence, and rarely rose to the bait when Benteen provoked him. Custer knew that Benteen, with all his spite and malevolence, was a fighting soldier and valued him as such. To Custer the soldier, the soldier was all that mattered. It is a pity that Custer had not been able to count on loyalty from Benteen.

Benteen's letter of February 22, 1896 to Goldin, written after twenty years of controversy over Custer and his last battle, plenty of time for evaluation and reflection by Benteen, is revealing of his character. His expansive bragging and self-praise were almost to the point of egomania; his self-opiniated remarks about how well he was liked, his prowess as a poker player and his personal bravery were smug. His malicious attitude toward those he disliked was also evident, illustrated in his gratuitous and slashing attack on General J. B. Fry. Benteen, sometimes almost hysterical in his character assassinations, slated Custer with snide remarks about his honesty and integrity, sneered at his writings and literary ability and impugned Custer's courage, even invoking the fact of Custer's stammer, an unfortunate impediment, to emphasise this.

Benteen wrote, "Sheridan always had an affection for me from the fact of giving twenty such good men and such an efficient Lieutenant to command his escort in '62 . . . There are many excellent ways of finding out the disposition and nature of a man . . . playing 'draw' with him . . . Thus I became acquainted with Custer. Ditto in the case of Gen. J. B. Fry . . . In the game of 'draw,' Fry thought no one from the old Vols had any right to down a Bvt. Major-General at the game, one who had studied philosophy and 'math' at the great National School: but at the same time I used to down him regularly . . . I hadn't a bit of respect for him if he was Adj. Gen. . . . by some hook or crook he had piled up a stack of coin of the realm. How?

"Hon Roscoe Conklin snubbed, and in the U.S. Senate denounced him, refusing always to speak to him, saying he wasn't clean and honest. Fry was a finical, cynical no end of all round d——n fool with an unlimited amount of brass and little else, though he thought he was an author, genius and all round grand man . . . Gen Hancock always seemed fond of me and was always kind, which was by no means the rule to everybody, being at times quite over-bearing I've been told. I never had an axe to grind.

"Mine was the only troop of cavalry left in New Orleans in '74 and '75 and when Sheridan came down to assume command he rather surprised Gen. Emory, 5th Cav. (then in command Dept. of the South) and E's staff, by the way he threw his arms around and hugged me, telling me he was glad I was there, and I know he was as I had made record in 1862 and he knew some of it . . . Custer at the time was foaming at the mouth at Lincoln. He was shut out of showing himself up in the newspapers; however he had the relaxation of giving to *The Galaxy* his *Lie on the Plains*.

"At Fort Cobb, Ind. Ter. in winter of '68–69, officers' call was sounded one night from Regt. Hdqtrs. I sauntered up, the other officers being mostly there when I arrived. The officers were squatted around the inside of Custer's Sibley tent (minus a wall), and Custer was walking around the centre of the tent with a rawhide riding whip in his hand. When all were assembled he went on with a rambling story, stammering the while, that it had been reported to him that someone or parties had been belittling the fight at the Washita &c., &c., and that if he heard any more of it, or it came to his ears who had done so, he would cowhide them, switching his rawhide the while. Being right at the door of the tent I stepped out drew my revolver, turned the cylinder to see that 'twas in good working order, returned it lightly to holster, and went within. At a pause in the talk I said, 'Gen. Custer. while I cannot father all of the blame you have asserted, still I guess I am the man you are after and I am ready for the whipping promised.' He stammered and said, 'Col. Benteen, I'll see you again, Sir!'

"Doubtless you can imagine what would have happened had the rawhide whirred! The 'call' broke up *sine die* in silence, but no tears from the whipping! I then went to Randolph Keim, reporter from *N.Y. Tribune* (the only man I had spoken to about the matter at all), and told him I wanted him to go with me at once to Custer's tent, taking his notes with him of all I had told him, as a whipping was due somebody and I didn't want a word I said omitted. Keim went with me, and though I'd told him enough, Custer wilted like a whipped cur.

"He evidently knew whom to whip! Now all of this kind of business was apt to result disastrously for me when Custer could so work it. But I was determined to 'stay right with' him; then the other fellows got a little more of men than formerly, and the Custer power can be said to have commenced to decline. Keim told Gen. Sheridan about the occurrence and Sheridan gave Custer a piece of his mind about the matter. (Sheridan knew that it was principally through me that Custer was then along, and he was rapidly beginning to learn to know more of the characteristics of the man, and I really think he cared little for him thereafter.)

"In 1876, when Custer came to Fort Lincoln with Terry, he found that Major Reno had divided the regiment into four battalions, captains commanding them. Custer at once changed that order, dividing regiment into two wings, Reno comdg. R. W. and I the left.

"Custer sent for me one day after the division of the rgt., and when at his tent (Mrs. Custer being there), he informed me that my cousin, Lawrence Cobright, had called him in Washington in spring of 1876 and wanted to know how I was getting along, seeming, Custer said, to be wonderfully interested in me. 'Yes,' said I, 'we've been very dear friends always.'

"Now Lawrence Cobright, during the whole war (and from the beginning of the Associated Press) had been at its head, its chief, and no despatches were given to the public by him affecting the Union cause until he had presented the same to President Lincoln and the Secretary of War, Stanton. Cobright, though a Southerner, was a Union man to the core, a democrat too, but as true as steel, and had the whole confidence of the President and Secretary through the whole of it. I then began to scent out the cause of the wing distribution by Custer. However, he had no idea of the pride of my race for at no time did I seek my preferment through Cobright's influence, and no one knew better than he that I would apply for none. However, he being the 'head-monk' of such a power, Custer perhaps feared that I might possibly bring influence to bear at some time. He was fully aware that I'd hold my own like a man and thought that perhaps he might need some such influence probably.

Pictograph made in 1881 by Chief Red Horse of the Seventh Cavalry dead at the Little Big Horn.

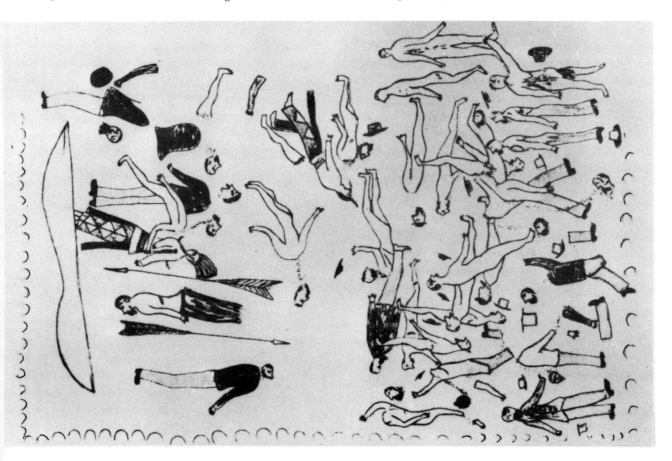

Martini, the last man to see Custer alive, on his retirement from the Seventh Cavalry as Sergeant Martin in 1904.

"Well, after the disaster, when curs of every grade were hounding Grant, Reno and myself, never did I write one word to Cobright. Had I, the matter would have gone to the world straight. You see, Colonel, there are wheels within wheels!"

In the twenty years following the death of Custer, far from mellowing it seemed that Benteen brooded over his grievances, enlarged imagined slights, built up a growing resentment of any criticism of his conduct, and grew ever more jealous of Custer, and this despite his own achievements against hostile Indians in this time, and promotion to General.

The events leading to the fight on the Little Big Horn are told by Benteen in his first narrative, written in his own hand fourteen years after the battle. This narrative gives a long-winded account about how he came to disobey Custer's orders regarding the disposal of guards for the pack train on the march, how he righteously explained it to Custer and how Custer sanctioned the changes Benteen had made. Benteen professed surprise that after officers' call, Custer should have given him and his troop the honour of the advance. But, with a changed situation, Benteen had been given instructions to move off with three troops of cavalry to a bluff two miles away on a scouting expedition. In the narrative Benteen is very wise with his premonitions made with hindsight. He said the first premonition he kept to himself; the second he acted upon, being detached from Custer's main body.

Regarding Martini, the trumpeter who had delivered the urgent "packs" message to him, Benteen said: "Martini, the trumpeter bringing this dispatch, was a thick headed, dull witted Italian just about as much cut out to be a cavalryman as he was for a king." Yet in 1923 in the *Cavalry Journal*, Lieutenant-Colonel W. A. Graham, relating the story of this very man, had a different opinion.

At the time of the Little Big Horn a man of twenty five, Martini was already the veteran of one war. He had been born in Rome in 1851 and named Giovanni Martini. At fourteen he had enlisted with Garibaldi as a drummer-boy in the Army of Liberation and had seen the backs of the Austrians at Villa Franca in '66. On his arrival in America in 1873 he had enlisted in the U.S. army and served continuously from 1874 to 1904 when he retired as Sergeant John Martin. Graham said that he was a remarkable old soldier. His Seventh Cavalry discharge, which he exhibited with pardonable pride, bore the signature of F. W. Benteen, his old troop commander, the man to whom Martini had conveyed Custer's last message, and Benteen had described Sergeant Martin in the discharge as the "only surviving witness of the Custer massacre." He made no mention of the man being a thick headed, dull witted Italian, and for a man Benteen had once described as "just about as much cut out to be a cavalryman as he was for a king," Martin had done well to last thirty years in the U.S. Cavalry.

94

The Custer legends

FREDERICK WHITTAKER WAS CUSTER'S FIRST BIOGRAPHER AND HIS BOOK, *Life of Gen. George A. Custer*, was a defence of the general. Whittaker unequivocally blamed Reno and Grant for Custer's death and castigated Benteen. He was lavish in his praise of his hero, eulogising him to a point where his passionate panegyrics were bound to cause violent reactions from the Custerphobes. Whittaker went overboard, comparing Custer to Caesar, Hannibal, Cromwell and Napoleon, and made syrupy allusions and references to Custer's boyhood and his courtship of Libbie Bacon. He glossed over Custer's faults in order to portray him as perfection, and crashed down on Reno, whom he indicted for having betrayed and deserted Custer. In his defence of Custer, Whittaker struck out hard in all directions and was often careless in his appraisals. He cast President Grant as a villain, arousing much indignation, and he in turn was lambasted cruelly. But Grant, hero of the Civil War though he may have been, was no paragon of virtue and Custer's partisanship in the attacks made on some of the crooked aspects of the Grant administration had certainly aroused the President's anger and bitterness. In the *New York Herald* on September 2, 1876 Grant stated that he regarded Custer's massacre as a sacrifice of troops brought on by Custer himself and wholly unnecessary.

Whittaker harshly charged that Grant had engineered Custer's death in revenge for Custer's sally into politics against him. Whittaker agitated for a court of inquiry to be set up to vindicate Custer and demanded that Congress investigate the charges against Reno. Reno, brutally pummelled over his performance at the Little Big Horn and hard-put to defend himself, was stung into demanding such an inquiry himself and one was convened in Chicago in January 1879. When Reno was cleared by the court, Whittaker lashed out in fury. In a letter to the *New York Sun* on February 26, 1879 he charged that the court's decision had been a "mockery of justice" and made scathing attacks on Reno, Benteen and even their counsel, charging not only that they ate and drank together at all times but that hotel loungers said they frequently slept three in a bed. What Whittaker meant to show in no uncertain manner was that Reno and Benteen were in collusion, and this was, more likely than not, true.

But Whittaker went too far in flaying Reno. Reno was forced to defend himself in any way he could. It was unfair deliberately to denigrate Reno in order to

Woodcut by W. M. Cary of
Custer's Last Stand, published
in a Manhattan newspaper on
July 19, 1876.

strengthen Custer's case. Custer did not need that. Whittaker's assertation that Reno had callously abandoned Custer because of cowardice was entirely wrong although that view has persisted in much of what has been written since 1876.

Whittaker was also responsible for the propagation of legends that grew out of the battle of the Little Big Horn. For example, he embellished the story of Curley the Crow surviving the battle and escaping hidden under a Sioux blanket, a tale that never did have much substance in the first place. Whittaker also repeated the legend that the Sioux Rain-in-the-Face, who was supposed to have sworn vengeance on Custer for once having him arrested, was actually the one who killed Custer. One story had Rain-in-the-Face cutting Custer's heart out, eating a slice of it and dancing around a pole with the heart stuck on it. But Custer's body had not been mutilated. Another story stated that the heart was that of Tom Custer, the general's brother. In his book *Outdoor Life*, published in March 1903, R. W. Kent wrote of a meeting he had with Rain-in-the-Face when the tamed Indian was appearing in a Wild West show on Coney Island and stated that he claimed that he killed Little Hair (presumably Tom Custer), saying, "I leaped from my pony and cut out his heart and bit a piece out of it and spit a piece of it in his face. I got back on my pony and rode off shaking it."

However, the honour of having killed Custer was claimed by many Indians, each claim begetting another legend. The truth is that the man who had killed Custer could have been any one of a thousand circling Indians closing in as Custer's depleted force was making its last stand. One theory, first suggested by Colonel Richard Dodge in *Our Wild Life Indians*, published in 1882, was that Custer, caught in a hopeless situation, shot himself. This was a possibility but not in keeping with Custer's temperament. In any case, Custer had been shot in the left temple and he had been right-handed. The battle is often called Custer's Last Stand, but of course, Custer might not have been the last man to go down. Custer standing defiantly alone, brandishing a sabre or firing a brace of pistols, amid the corpses of his gallant troopers and hosts of triumphant Indians, is another legend.

Whittaker was savagely mauled in his turn by critics. His biography was said to be a nineteenth century version of the life of a medieval saint. Perhaps to Whittaker, Custer was a saint. Persons have been canonised for less virtues than Whittaker saw in his hero.

Custer and his wife had idolised one another and after his death, Libbie, articulate and dedicated, soon made nonsense of the old saying that "no man is a hero to his wife." In her books, *Boots and Saddles* and *Following the Guidon* she had nothing but paeans of praise for her beloved husband. To her he had been the embodiment of all that was good and noble, the epitome of all manly virtues, yet in sentimental tales, poignant reminiscences and anecdotes she painted an idealised picture of Custer which made him appear almost androgynous at times with the plethora of saintly attributes she found in him. For the doting Mrs. Custer her husband and lover had also been the sons and daughters they had never had.

Using Custer and his career as a basis, writers wrote works of fiction full of imaginative exploits, theories and non sequiturs which often crept out from the realms of fiction into the world of the Custer controversy, blurring the hard edges of truth and creating new legends and myths to reappear in books thereafter.

As controversy raged, legend grew. Buffalo Bill Cody, the scout, a born showman who had always considered Custer a man after his own heart, helped to enhance the magic of Custer legend in his own stories and autobiography which appeared in 1879, as well as in his successful Wild West show which he organised in 1883 and took to Europe in 1887. The show featured as a dramatic finale a re-enactment of Custer's Last Stand.

William Frederick Cody, Buffalo Bill, was himself a legend and a folk hero. Cody had served as an army scout and guide in the Civil War, and in the Sioux War of 1876 on July 17 at the Battle of Indian Creek he killed Chief Yellow Hand of the Cheyennes in personal combat. Lifting his scalp, Buffalo Bill had yelled, "The first scalp for Custer." Soon, an account of his fight appeared in a dime novel entitled *The Crimson Trail; on Custer's Last Warpath*, and in subsequent dime novels under Cody's own name. The incident was even featured in a stage melodrama, *The Red Right Hand; or Buffalo Bill's First Scalp for Custer*. Stories in boys' papers such as *Beadle's Boys' Library* kept alive interest in the romance of the West and Western heroes such as Davy Crockett and Kit Carson as well as notorious characters including Wild Bill Hickok, Wyatt Earp and Billy the Kid and complemented stories about Custer, perpetuating his legend.

Mrs. Laura Webb wrote a maudlin poem on *Custer's Immortality* and later Captain Jack Crawford, frontier scout and homespun poet, added his contribution, and even notable poets such as Henry Wadsworth Longfellow, John Greenleaf Whittier and Ella Wheeler Wilcox wrote poems about Custer's Last Stand.

Writers impregnating fact with fiction put words into the mouths of their heroes and villains to voice their own sentiments and views about Custer. One of these writers was Cyrus Townsend Brady, prolific in his output of fiction and historical accounts of the West; others were Herbert Myrick and Randall Parish. Each painted a portrait of Custer according to his own lights. All the same, somehow Custer always managed to emerge as a more absorbing character than any imagined character in these books, where more often than not the historical threads of the plot were not only stretched to breaking point but broken beyond repair.

Later biographers of Custer like Frederick Dellenbaugh, author of *George Armstrong Custer*, published in 1917, and Frazier Hunt who wrote *The Last of the Cavaliers* in 1928, have been criticised for failing to analyse and delineate what critics decided was the complexity of Custer's character and for adhering to what was called the nineteenth century tradition of frank hero worship. But all was not lost to the scalp hunters. In 1934, Van de Winter in his *Glory Hunter*, at a time when it was becoming increasingly fashionable to debunk heroes, jumped

Rain-in-the-Face told highly
coloured stories of his part in
the great battle.

on the bandwagon and galloped way back West armed to the teeth with the latest weapons of psychological warfare to mow down the mellower memories of Custer. Other iconoclasts were quick to mount up and follow Van de Winter with wild whoops, waving tomahawks to chop Custer to bits.

Van de Winter twisted everything that could possibly be twisted to portray Custer as arrogant, impetuous and irresponsible and as an incompetent young jumped-up fool who was utterly devoid of compassion. He scoffed at Custer's exploits and denied him any military skill. He twisted his material so much that sometimes he unwittingly twisted some of it back into shape. He saw Custer's buffalo hunting exploits as proof of cruelty and sadism, a theme inevitably taken up by other writers. But Custer lived on lands where hunting for meat to eat was normal and necessary and where also it was common for some buffalo hunters to slaughter whole herds of the animals for their skins alone, leaving the carcasses to rot while Indians starved. Certainly there was nothing squeamish about the soldier Custer, who had seen men blown to bits in battle, seen the remains of men who had been scalped and mutilated by Indians, seen men, women and children stinking in various stages of decomposition. He who had been directed by his Government to kill Indians and to be dispassionate about it could hardly be expected to show a good deal of conscience in drawing the line between butchery in sport and butchery for eating. Fraternities of today, which include women, hunt for pleasure and show no aversion when a fox is torn to pieces by dogs.

Yet one writer accused Custer of sadism over an episode, recounted by Mrs. Custer, where Custer wounded a buffalo and then waited for the women of the party to hurry up to see him deliver the coup-de-grace in much the same manner as in a present day foxhunt. And those women were tough pioneers of the West, not the products of the best finishing schools of Europe.

Perhaps Custer was as Van de Winter portrayed him, but if it were so there has never been a particle of hard evidence to prove it. For a man who was purported to be cruel, Custer treated his dogs and pets, which at one time included a pelican and a wildcat, very well indeed, and there is evidence to prove that.

The other writers who gleefully followed de Winter with their various Frankenstein concoctions featured Custer as a second rate prima donna or a bundle of complicated neuroses. But their works were more or less fiction and any similarity to real characters or events past or present was in names and places only, and it is not necessary to read these works thoroughly to discover this. However this Custerphobia in no way detracts from the quality of the writing, the plot or interest of many such novels. *Bugles in the Afternoon* by Ernest Haycox, published in 1944 and filmed in 1952, is an eminently readable story but the words referring to Custer that issue from the mouths of the characters are, of course, fiction broadly based on mere rumour and the interpretations are biased.

In *Fighting Indians of the West* by Martin Schnitt and Dee Brown, published in

1948, Custer was depicted as a nasty, sneaky selfseeker who could not defeat the Indians in a fair fight. What the authors would have regarded as fair fighting conjures up visions of a public school quadrangle in old England with stiff upper lipped schoolboys playing cowboys and Indians and bashing each other to bits shouting, "Yah! Sucks! Boo!" and "Fair dos, you cads!"

Most novelists of recent years featuring Custer, found some particular facet of his career that could be rendered unsavoury, to blow up to major proportions and use as the main theme for a book, possibly with the hypothesis that everyone likes to hate and see a hero destroyed. For instance, Clay Fisher in his novel *Yellow Hair*, published in 1954, fastens on the story embellished by Benteen in his letters to Goldin about Custer and the Indian girl, Monahseeta, captured at Washita, by whom it was bruited that Custer had a child, fair-headed like himself. To serve the purpose of this far-fetched novel, Custer is cast in the role of villain.

Will Henry's *No Survivors* (1950) is fiction. The vehement anti-Custer dissertations are strong stuff but with no back-up and the words in the mouths of the characters in Kenneth Shifflet's *Convenient Coward* (1961) are cartoon balloons, romanticising for the sake of romanticising, sounding about as plausible as the words put into the mouths of the "ordinary man in the street" in party political broadcasts. In 1957 David Humphreys Miller had a go at Custer, using garbled tales of Indian survivors of the Little Big Horn as his big stick to beat Custer. A biography of Custer by Jay Monaghan which appeared in 1959 adopted a middle of the road approach in assessing the career of Custer. This was considered somewhat unusual, as partisanship in the case of Custer is usually unequivocal. In Alvin Joseph's *Patriotic Chiefs*, published in 1961, which purported to be a history of Indian leadership, Custer again came in for a caning. It was stated, against all evidence, that it was Custer the glory hunter's irascible behaviour and bad treatment of his men that caused them to desert. Also, to cast Custer as a villain in order to evince sympathy for the Plains Indians was poor casting indeed when there were so many policy makers who classed all Indians as vermin to be exterminated, to choose from.

Another writer who, in his zeal to side with the Indians, fixed on the idea that Custer was their merciless enemy, was Charles J. Brill. In his *Conquest of the Southern Plains*, published in 1938, Custer was shown as vicious, treacherous, and lying in his dealings with Indians as well as with his own troops. Moreover, Brill also cracked the skin of Benteen's old chestnut, the story about the illicit affair between Custer and Monahseeta, complete with the resultant yellow-haired baby.

It is strange that Benteen should ever have spread the story of Monahseeta It is possible he envied Custer's popularity with the ladies, equating it with sexuality, and the fact that Custer had a beautiful, doting wife. In a letter to his own wife written on July 25, a month after Custer's death, Benteen wrote, "I had a queer dream of Col. Keogh the night before last, 'twas that he would insist upon undressing in the room in which you were. I had to give him a 'dressing'

Indian warrior; illustration
by Frederic Remington.

Frederic Remington

Custer's Last Stand, from an
original painting in the Karl
May Indian Museum in
Dresden, Germany.

Custer rides again in an
improbable story in a
Spanish comic book.

to cure him of the fancy. I rarely ever thought of the man—and 'tis queer I should have dreamt of him."

Not so queer. In this dream, Keogh, killed at the Little Big Horn, replaces Custer in a position with sexual connotations, which consciously Benteen would never bear to think about. Probably Benteen would have liked Custer to have shown some interest in Mrs. Benteen so that he could have felt that he had something which Custer wanted.

Naturally the advent of the cinema was bound to bring Custer to the screen. The Custer story was a ready made Western saga with enough advance publicity to make any movie maker brimful of joy and was a subject that could be repeated one way or another for years to come. Nobody has yet made *The Son of Custer*, *The Bride of Custer* and *Custer meets Frankenstein*. In 1909, *Custer's Last Stand*, a one-reeler, was made by Colonel William Selig, and in 1912 Thomas H. Ince produced *Custer's Last Fight*. Clara Bow, the famous "It" girl, and Johnny Walker starred in *Scarlet West* which was about Custer. Custer was featured in *Flaming Frontier* with Dustin Farnum in 1926, and *Custer's Last Stand* was a movie serial with fifteen episodes, appearing in 1936 with Frank McGlynn Jr. as Custer. This was pure fiction, with white renegades helping the Indians against Custer. Custer featured in *Santa Fe Trail* in 1940, which starred the later Governor of California, Ronald Reagan, and in *The Badlands of Dakota* in 1941, with Addison Richards. Errol Flynn was a natural for the role of Custer and sure enough there he was in *They Died with Their Boots On* in 1942. In this telescoped version of Custer's life and death his career at West Point was cleverly worked into the plot. Olivia De Havilland playing Libbie was enough to turn any Custerphobe into a Custerphile and Errol Flynn dying nobly amidst piles of clinical dead at the Little Big Horn was a credit to Custer's memory.

In 1952 *Bugles in the Afternoon* was made into a film with Sheb Wooley and in 1954 came *Sitting Bull*, which portrayed the famous Sioux medicine man as a noble leader who was crossed, double-crossed and triple-crossed by a dastardly Custer, who was determined to ignore all efforts for peace because of a psychopathic hatred of Indians. *Tonka*, with Britt Lomond, made by Walt Disney in 1957, was about as fanciful as his *Snow White and the Seven Dwarfs*, Custer appearing again as a sadistic Indian-hater, petulant and self-opinioned. In 1966 came Robert Shaw in *Custer of the West* with Mary Ure, Robert Ryan, Ty Hardin and Jeffrey Hunter. The pay-off came with Custer standing alone on the field of glory being offered honourable surrender by Sitting Bull but choosing to go down fighting. Was there the sound of celestial bugles? *Little Big Man*, 1970. with Dustin Hoffman, Martin Balsam and Faye Dunaway, was about an Indian, one hundred and twenty years old, who claimed to be the sole survivor of the Battle of the Little Big Horn. Other films in which Custer was portrayed were *The Fighting 7th* in 1952 and *The Seventh Cavalry* in 1957.

There was a short-lived television series called *Custer* in 1968, made by 20th Century Fox and starring Wayne Maunder, in which Custer was just the launching pad for a routine "oater." All in all, so far on the screen, Custer has never been more than a simulacrum.

Artists got into the Custer act with dozens of impressions of the "Last Stand," and many were not too fussy about their representations, paying little attention to detail and authenticity. A woodcut by W. M. Carey, appearing in the *New York Graphic Illustrated* newspaper, was the first attempt to depict the Battle of the Little Big Horn which had taken place just three weeks previously and in August 1876 in Whittaker's *Life of Custer* there was the illustration, *Custer's Last Fight*, by A. K. Waud.

For the next two or three decades, artists scratched and daubed with oils, watercolours and inks using Custer's Last Stand as their inspiration with varying degrees of quality and accuracy. In 1881 John Mulvany painted *Custer's Last Rally*, but the most famous portrayal was the famous *Last Fight* by Cassily Adams painted in 1886. Lithographs of it by Otto Becker were later distributed to 150,000 saloons all over the United States by Anheuser-Busch to advertise their beer and were seen by millions of customers.

Custer's Last Stand by King and Allison looks like a painting of an ill-assorted bunch of toy soldiers surrounded by a collection of wooden cigar store Indians on horseback, and a grotesque painting by James R. Meyer is reminiscent of the children at school. One of the most deftly accurate reconstructions of the battle is a painting in the Whitney Gallery of Western Art at Cody, Wyoming. It is a canvas painted in 1899 by Edgar Paxon after twenty years of research, it is said. Although a sick looking trooper sitting up blowing a bugle in the midst of all the hullabaloo does seem a bit off, the figures look realistic enough.

Even European artists have found inspiration in the Custer Legend. *Custer's Last Stand* by Elk Eber, *The Final Rush* by Linde Berg, and *Sitting Bull Receiving the Message "We Have Killed Them All"* are original paintings, all in the Karl May Indian Museum, Dresden, Germany. Illustrators in black and white, too, such as Mick Anglo, Don Lawrence and Frank Bellamy, have used a stylised Custer as a subject for strip cartoons.

Colonel W. A. Graham, Custer expert and author, whose *The Custer Myth, A Source Book of Custeriana* is a masterpiece, described Fred Dustin of Michigan, author of *The Custer Tragedy* as a master of research and, as far as technical research is concerned, there is no doubt about that. But Dustin was an "if" man and "if" has no place in history. Dustin propounded that the Little Big Horn would have been a victory *if* Custer had obeyed orders, and that presumed that he had not. But "if" has no meaning. Like, "if Custer, not Terry, had been given overall command of the campaign, Custer would have been victorious."

Again comes the question whether or not Custer disobeyed Terry's orders. Just suppose he did not. History is full of heroes who disobeyed orders or acted on their own interpretations of orders and won glory. Nelson turned his blind eye and a huge statue in Trafalgar Square commemorates him. Were the orders from a general such as Terry all that sacrosanct, anyway? Was Terry a better general than Custer? Custer had only been replaced by Terry because a fatted

Grant had been infuriated by Custer's foray into the political field.

Orders can be wrong; orders can be interpreted in different ways and sometimes altered circumstances make it wise to ignore orders. The chances are that more men have gone to their death because of blind obedience to stupid or inflexible orders than have for disobeying them. That is not to say that Terry's orders were stupid, but they were equivocal in some respects and lacked clarity in others. That could have been intentional. However, Custer was given the field and leave to decide his actions. He decided according to conditions prevailing at the time in the war zone and died, his men with him.

Whatever the circumstances of his judgment, his leadership, his interpretation of orders, implied disobedience and recklessness, Custer had sought the action which was the reason for Terry's force being in the field. He had fought gallantly against odds to the end and his glory cannot be denied. No Benteen could shatter that for it was no illusion. Custer, Benteen's bête noir, was and is forever a hero.

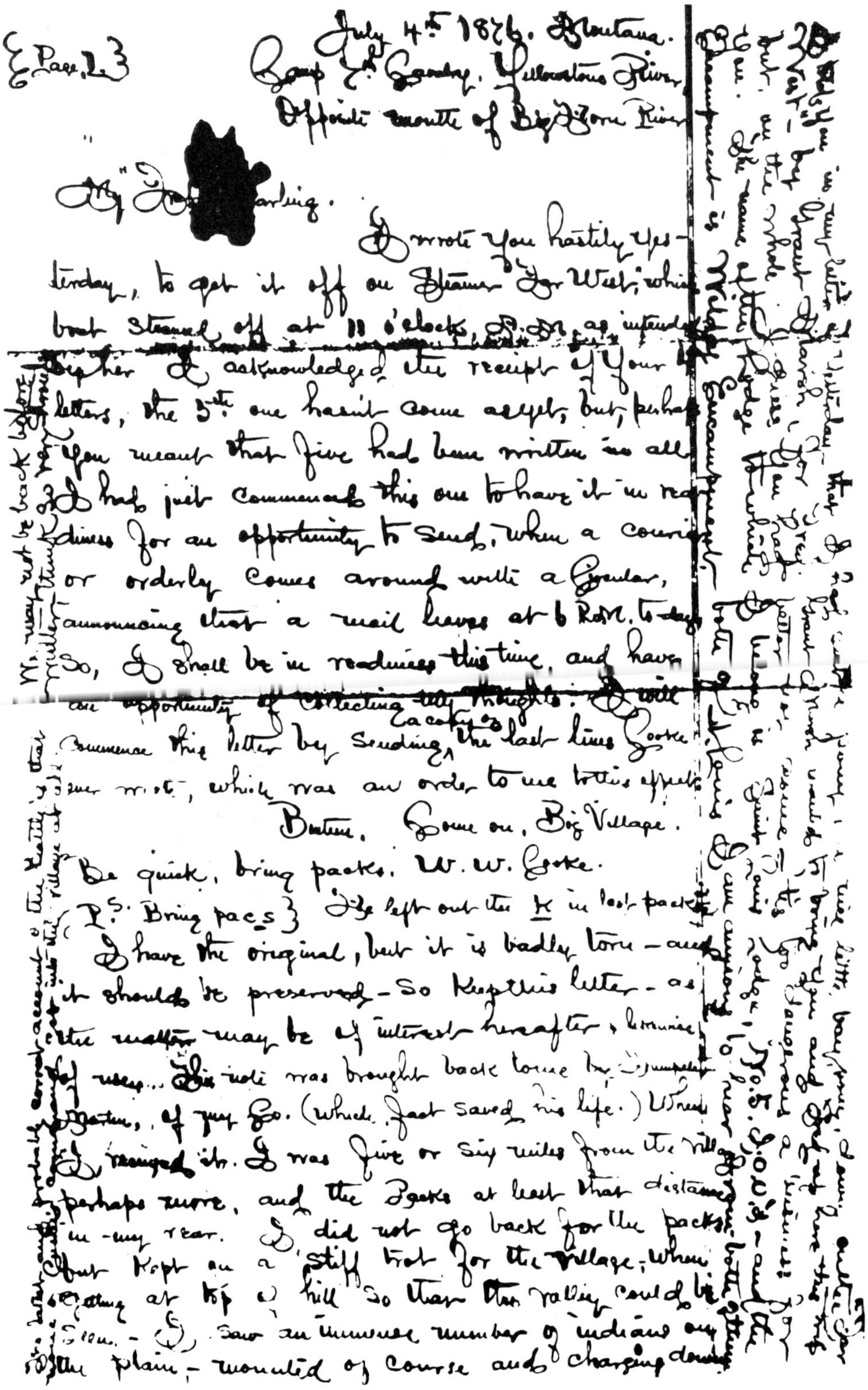

Benteen's letter to his wife in
1876 (text opposite).

Appendix

BENTEEN'S LETTER TO HIS WIFE

July 4th 1876, Montana,
Camp 7th Cavalry, Yellowstone River,
Opposite mouth of Big Horn River.

My Darling,   I will commence this letter by sending a copy of the last lines Cooke ever wrote, which was an order to me to this effect: "Benteen. Come on. Big village. Be quick, bring packs.   W. W. Cooke. (P. S. Bring pac-s)."

He left out the "k" in last packs.   I have the original, but it is badly torn and it should be preserved. So keep this letter, as the matter may be of interest hereafter, likewise of use. This note was brought back to me by Trumpeter Martin of my Co. (which fact saved his life.) When I received it I was five or six miles from the village, perhaps more, and the packs at least that distance in my rear. I did not go back for the packs but kept on a stiff trot for the village. When getting at top of hill so that the valley could be seen—I saw an immense number of Indians on the plain, mounted of course and charging down on some dismounted men of Reno's command; the balance of R's command were mounted, and flying for dear life to the bluffs on the same side of river that I was. I then marched my 3 Co's. to them and a more delighted lot of folks you never saw.

To commence—On the 22nd of June—Custer, with the 7th Cavalry left the Steamer "Far West," Genl. Terry and Genl. Gibbon's command (which latter was then in on the side of river and in same camp in which we now are) and moved up the Rosebud, marching 12 miles—the next day we marched 35 miles up the same stream. The next day we marched 35 more miles up same stream and went into bivouac, remaining until 12 o'clock P. M. We then marched until about daylight, making about 10 miles; about half past five we started again— and after going 6 or 7 miles we halted and officers' call was sounded. We were asked how many men of the companies were with the Co. Packs and instructed that only six could remain with them—and the discourse wound up with—that we should see that the men were supplied with the quantity of ammunition as had been specified in orders and that the 1st Co. that reported itself in readiness should be the advance Co. I knew that my Co. was in the desired condition and

109

it being near the point of Assembly I went to it, assured myself of same, then announced to Genl. Custer that "H" Co. was ready; he replied the Advance is yours, Col. Benteen.

We then moved four or five miles and halted between the slopes of two hills and the Regt. was divided into Battalions—Reno getting Co's. "A. G. and M." I getting "D. H. K." From that point I was ordered with my Battn. to go over the immense hills to the left, in search of the valley, which was supposed to be very near by and to pitch into anything I came across—and to inform Custer at once if I found anything worthy of same. Well, I suppose I went up and down those hills for 10 miles—and still no valley anywhere in sight, the horses were fast giving out from steady climbing—and as my orders had been fulfilled I struck diagonally for the trail the command had marched on, getting to it just before the Pack train got there—or on the trail just ahead of it. I then marched rapidly and after about 6 or 7 miles came upon a burning tepee—in which was the body of an Indian on a scaffold, arrayed gorgeously—None of the command was in sight at this time. The ground from this to the valley was descending but very rough. I kept up my trot and when I reached a point very near the ford which was crossed by Reno's Battn. I got my first sight of the Valley and river—and Reno's command in full flight for the bluffs to the side I was then on—Of course I joined them at once. The ground where Reno charged on was a plain 5 or 6 miles or 10 miles long and about one mile or more wide; Custer sent him in there and promised to support him—after Reno started in, Custer with his five Co's instead of crossing the ford went to the right—around some high bluffs—with the intention—as is supposed—of striking the rear of the village; from the bluff on which he got he had his first glimpose of the whole of it—and I can tell you 'twas an immense one.

From that point Cooke sent the note to me by Martin, which I have quoted on 1st page. I suppose after the five Co's had closed up somewhat Custer started down for the village, all throats bursting themselves with cheering (So says Martin). He had 3½ or 4 miles to go before he got to a ford—as the Village was on the plain on opposite side to Custer's column. So, when he got over those 4 miles of rough country and reached the ford, the Indians had availed themselves of the timely information given by the cheering—as to the whereabouts and intentions of that column, and had arrangements completed to receive it. Whether the Indians allowed Custer's column to cross at all, is a mooted question, but I am of the opinion that nearly—if not all of the five companies got into the village—but were driven out immediately—flying in great disorder and crossing by two instead of the one ford by which they entered. "E" Co. going by the left and "F. I. and L." by the same one they crossed. What became of "C" Co. no one knows—they must have charged there below the village, gotten away—or have been killed in the bluffs on the village side of stream—as very few of "C" Co. horses are found. Jack Sturgis and Porter's clothes were found in the Village. After the Indians had driven them across, it was a regular buffalo hunt for them and not a man escaped. We buried 203 of the bodies of Custer's command the 2d day after fight—The bodies were as recognisable as if they were in life. With Custer—was Keogh, Yates and Tom Custer (3 Captains) 1st Lieut's. Cooke, A. E. Smith, Porter, Calhoun (4) 2d Lieuts. Harrington, Sturgis, Riley and Crittenden (J. J. of 20th Inf.) Asst. Surgeon Lord was along—but his body was not recognised. Neither was Porter's not Sturgis' nor Harrington's.

McIntosh and Hodgson were killed at Reno's end of line—in attempting to get back to bluffs. DeRudio was supposed to have been lost, but the same night the Indians left their village he came sauntering in dismounted, accompanied by McIntosh's cook. They had hidden away in the woods. He had a thrilling romantic story made out already—embellished, you bet! The stories of O'Neill (the man who was with him) and De R's of course, couldn't be expected to agree, but far more of truth, I am inclined to think, will be found in the narrative of O'Neill; at any rate, it is not at all colored—as he is a cool, level-headed fellow—and tells it plainly *and the same way all the time*—which is a big thing towards convincing one of the truth of a story.

I must now tell you what we did—When I found Reno's command. We halted for the packs to come up—and then moved along the line of bluffs towards the direction Custer was supposed to have gone in. Weir's Company was sent out to communicate with Custer, but it was driven back. We then showed our full force on the hills with Guidons flying, that Custer might see us—but we could see nothing of him, couldn't hear much firing, but could see immense body of Indians coming to attack us from both sides of the river. We withdrew to a saucer like hill, putting our horses and packs in the bottom of saucer and threw all of our force dismounted around this corral; the animals could be riddled from only one point—but we had not men enough to extend our line to that—so we could not get it—therefore the Indians amused themselves by shooting at our stock, ditto, men—but they, the men, could cover themselves. Both of my horses (U. S. horses) were wounded. Well they pounded at us all of what was left of the 1st day and the whole of the 2d day—withdrawing their line with the withdrawal of their village, which was at dusk the 2d day. Corporal Loll, Meador and Jones were killed; Sergt. Pahl, both of the Bishops, Phillips, Windolph, Black, Severs, Cooper, etc. (21 altogether) wounded. I got a slight scratch on my right thumb, which, as you see, doesn't prevent me from writing you this long scrawl. As this goes via Fort Ellis it will be a long time reaching you. Genl. Terry, with Genl. Gibbon's command—came up the morning of the 3d day, about 10 o'clock. Indians had all gone the night before. Had Custer carried out the orders he got from Genl. Terry, the commands would have formed a junction exactly at the village, and have captured the whole outfit of tepees, etc. and probably any quantity of squaws, papooses, etc. but Custer disobeyed orders from the fact of not wanting any other command—or body to have a finger in the pie—and thereby lost his life. (3000 warriors were there).

Well—Wifey Darling, I think this will do for a letter, so with oceans of love to you and Fred and kisses innumerable, I am devotedly, Your husband

FRED BENTEEN

October 20, 1891

It is very gratifying to know that my efforts while belonging to the 7th Cavalry were appreciated by the rank and file—i.e., the enlisted men—and your letter of today tells me that they were.

I was with the regiment from its organisation to December 1882, and of course can look far behind the date you came to me, and the backward glance is as full of memories—many of them glorious, and all pleasant, as from the point where you first drew saber. Capt. Owen Hale was the last of our old "mess" of seven to bite the dust, and I alone remain to think of them; I mean the mess association and cherish their memories in that regard.

In 1866 I could have gone into the 10th U. S. Cavalry as a Major but I preferred a Captaincy in the Seventh. Fate, however, after being a Captain 17 years, threw me into a negro organisation of cavalry anyhow; and being well off in this world's goods, and feeling that it was not proper to remain with a race of troops that I could take no interest in—and having served my 30 years—there seemed nothing to do but to commence looking after my property interests.

It cost me $10,000 more than my pay came to, to follow the trumpet calls of the United States, and this amount was not thrown away or wasted, either. Now, as a retired Major, I am getting along comfortably, and am looking after my flocks and herds—city blocks in prospective—and the interests of Fred, my only child. I lost four children in following that brazen trumpet around.

I am pleased, my dear sir, at having heard from you, and I wish you an uninterrupted run of everything that is good.

November 10, 1891

It pleases me to know that you knew and liked Lieut. Aspinwall of the 7th Cavalry—for he was a good fellow. I was commanding the post of Fort Rice, D.T., and appointed Aspinwall Assistant Commissary of Subsistence, which office, having funds, ready cash, monthly, completed what was begun in (by?) Custer's coterie in 1869, and ended the army career of poor John.

Capt. E. S. Godfrey wrote to me when I was at Fort McKinney, Wyoming, in 1886, about an article he was engaged at for a magazine concerning the 1876 campaign; my answer to him was to the effect, "That the greatest of these was charity," and asked him if he didn't think Reno had been sufficiently damned?

Pretty nearly ever since the stepping down and out of the more prominent actors in that fight of ours, June 25–26, 1876, Godfrey has been trying to make much capital for himself; and perhaps 'twas well that he didn't undertake to do it sooner. Of course I knew a great many things about the fight that 'tisn't essential that the world should know; "qui bono?" but I shouldn't like to see Godfrey attempt to parade himself as an at all prominent actor in it. I don't suppose there was ever an officer of the army got such a "cussing out" as I gave Mathey at the L. Big Horn on the eve of June 25th, and before crowds of enlisted men, officers and "packs". Personally, I brought three of the mules of the train back—the mules being loaded with ammunition, and had gotten quite a long way down toward the water, for which they were heading, before I could "round them up." Everybody—I mean most of the captains and all of the subalterns in the 7th, seemed to be positively afraid of Custer. However, without parade, when he did anything that was irregular to me, or infringed on "regulations," where I was concerned, I always went to him in "propria persona" and had the matter adjusted at once. Custer liked me for it, and I always surmised what I afterwards learned, de facto, that he wanted me badly as a friend; but I could not be, tho' I never fought him covertly.

Reno and Weir were never friendly, but the cause of this I never inquired or knew. What was the conversation between Reno and Weir on the little knoll on the bluffs? Weir belonged to my battalion, and, as I always thought, to "show his smartness" sallied out without orders on the march down the river; however, he was glad enough to have us pull his troop (out of?) there and back, and he played a very humble part in the fight till 'twas well closed.

Should you seen anything, or hear more of an article from Godfrey, be kind enough to let me know.

BENTEEN'S NARRATIVE

ON JUNE 22D, 1876, THE 7TH UNITED STATES CAVALRY, THEN ON THE Yellowstone River, Montana Territory, passed in review, guidons fluttering, horses prancing, before Brevet Major General A. H. Terry, commanding then the Department of Dakota, Headquarters in the Field; the 7th was en route, where? none knew of the Regt. but General G. A. Custer. However, I have since been informed by Brevet Major General John Gibbon, who was of the reviewing party, that his last salutation to General Custer was "Now, don't be greedy Custer, as there are Indians enough for all of us"!

On that day we moved up the "Rosebud," marching twelve (12) miles, and bivouacked: in the evening the orderly trumpeter was sent to notify the officers of the regiment that Genl. Custer wished to see them at his headquarters, and after arrival of the last officer, General Custer commenced his talk, which was to the effect that it had come to his knowledge that his official action had been criticised by some of the officers of the regiment at headquarters of the Department, and that while he was willing to accept recommendations from the junior second lieutenant of the regiment, he wished the same to come in a proper manner, calling our attention to the paragraph of Army Regulations referring

9.) was put in advance of it; one troop on the right flank of centre of train, nearest the hills; and the remaining troop in the rear of train... the march that day was 35 miles. — Some little while before reaching bivouac of regiment, I missed Dr. Lord from my side, he having accompanied me on the march for the two days. —

10. — However, on arrival at bivouac, the Adjutant of Regt. 3rd Cav. _____ came out to indicate place of bivouac for each troop, to have it in its proper order for marching on next day: after learning which, I said, "See here, Cookey, G. A. C. ordered me to march the 3 troops of the battalion composing guard for "packs," in rear of the last mule of train; now as the C. O. of Regt. told us last night that he was open for recommendations &c., I tell you as adjutant of regiment, that the first thing we know, some Casabianca

11. — will be getting such orders about the train, and if the roughness of the country holds out, and the indian signs continue to thicken why, the train will go up there, the circus adjourn — I am willing to show this was getting close upon infracting the paragraph of Army Regulations to which our attention had been invited on the evening previous; but I was telling it to the adjutant that it might be sandwiched in as if were in conversation with the commanding officer of the regiment, and I knew if he did

12. — that I would not be put in the light of a fault finder, but that in more elegant language the spirit of my talk would be given and perhaps might call the attention of the General to a matter that might mar the success of the campaign: however the Adjt. refused, point blank, to _____ anything about it to Custer, saying, I might tell him myself if I chose; so, the next morning as General Custer was passing, Jack to do so; telling him, that I could not, without endangering the safety of the command carry out the orders he

to the criticism of actions of commanding officers; and said he would take the necessary steps to punish, should there be reoccurence of the offence.

I said to General Custer, it seems to me you are lashing the shoulders of *all*, to get at some; now, as we are all present, would it not do to specify the officers whom you accuse? He said, Colonel Benteen, I am not here to be catechised by you, but for your own information, will state that none of my remarks have been directed towards you. Then, after giving a few excellent general orders as to what should be done by each troop of the regiment in case of an attack on our bivouac at any time, the meeting of the officers was over, and each adjourned to his palatial "Pup tent." On the next day, owing to the report of the lieutenant having control of the marching of the pack-train, the mules or packers of my troop having been reported with two other troops as being the most unmanageable in the regiment, I was directed to assume command of those three troops, and to march the battalion in rear of the last mule of the train. I saluted the General, and awaited the opportunity of crossing the Rosebud in rear of the regiment: it took exactly one hour and thirty minutes to get that pack-train across the creek, and get it started on other side:—The country through which we were marching was very broken, and over ravines that would have concealed thousands of Indians, so, after marching, say seven or eight miles, and the train being scattered for perhaps two miles, it occurred to me that perhaps the Casabianca business might be over construed, and that the pack train had better be "Rounded up," or I might have a knotty explanation to grind out should it be lost, which was one of the easiest of things to have happen, as I was marching. So, a trumpeter quickly galloped ahead with orders to halt the train, and on arrival of the battalion at the train, one troop of battalion was put in advance of it, one troop on the right flank of centre of train, nearest the hills, and the remaining troop in the rear of train. The march that day was 35 miles. Some littlewhile before reaching bivouac of regiment, I missed Dr. Lord from my side, he having accompanied me on the march for the two days. However, on arrival at bivouac, the Adjutant of Regt. 1st Lieut. W. W. Cooke, came out to indicate place of bivouac for each troop, to have it in its proper order for marching on next day: after learning which, I said, See here, "Cookey," "G. A. C." ordered me to march the 3 troops of the battalion composing guard for "packs," in rear of the last mule of train; now as the C. O. of Regt. told us last night that he was open for recommendations, &c., I tell you as adjutant of regiment, that the first thing we know, some Casabianca will be getting such orders about the train, and if the roughness of the country holds out, and the Indian signs continue to thicken, why, the train will go up, then, the circus adjourns.

I am willing to admit this was getting close upon infracting the paragraph of Army Regulations to which our attention had been invited on the evening previous; but I was telling it to the adjutant that it might be sandwiched in as it were in conversation with the commanding officer of the regiment, and I knew if he did that I would not be put in the light of a fault-finder, but that in more elegant language the spirit of my talk would be given, and perhaps might call the

attention of the General to a matter that might mar the success of the campaign. However, the Adjt. refused, point blank, to say anything about it to Custer, saying, I might tell him myself if I chose. So, the next morning as General Custer was passing, I chose to do so; telling him, that I could not, without endangering the safety of the packs, carry out the orders he had given me concerning the marching of the battalion composing the "Packs" guard. I then told the arrangement I had made of the battalion; and this from the fact that from the time he left me at the bivouac of the night before, not one sight of his command had been gotten. The General said, I am much obliged to you Colonel, and I will turn over the same order of march for the rear guard to the officer who relieves you.

Well, after the 2d day's march, and I had seen to the bivouacking of my troop, I got out my seine for purpose of seeing the kinds of fish the Rosebud could set up for supper. The attempt however resulted mostly in "water-hauls," and being ravenously hungry, "S.O.B. and trimmings," had to serve for bill of fare. Dr. Lord not putting in an appearance at the meal, however, after I had crawled under a bullberry bush for sweet repose, the Dr. came into camp, telling me that he had halted alone some miles back, being completely tired out, broken down, so much so that he had given up all hopes of getting to camp. He declined tea, and wanted nothing to eat or drink. I state this to show what must have been the physical condition of the Doctor on June 25th, on going into the fight, after an almost continuous march of 84 miles.

The repose I found under the bullberry bush alluded to, can be classed with the goose egg of the cricketer, for there were myriads of mosquitoes under that bush when I got there, and I don't think that any of them got away.

1st night's loss of sleep.

3rd day we marched to, strange to say, a creek called "Muddy Creek," where, on coming into camp I heard the voice of my old friend Col. Myles W. Keogh hailing me, saying, come here "old man," I've kept the nicest spot in the whole camp next to me, for your troop, & I've had to bluff the balance to hold it, but here it is, skip off," so I "skipped," putting my troop in the vale the gallant Irishman had held for me.

It wasn't far from twilight then, so, after getting supper Keogh came over to my bullberry bush, (he was more luxurious than I was, having a tent fly for shelter) and the crowd was listening to one of the Italian patriot, De Rudio's recitals, of his hair breadth scapes with Mazzini, or some other man, in some other country, all of which I rudely interrupted by saying, See here, fellows, you want to be collecting all the sleep you can, and be doing it soon, for I have a "Pre." that we are not going to stay in this camp tonight, but we are going to march all night, so, good-night. I had scarcely gotten the words from my lips before the orderly trumpeter notified us that we would meet at the commanding officer's headquarters at once: my preparations for sleep consisted in putting off my cavalry boots, so little time was consumed in robing: However, that was sufficient, the other officers rapidly went to their summons, it being quite dark there, and the "Pre." telling me 'twas a move. I called up my 1st Sergeant, and

117

had him see that the aparejos were "O.K." ropes, bridles, &c., all right, and have everything ready about the troop for a speedy move.

I then commenced a search for the Head Quarters; however, before getting far, I met an officer returning from the "Call," saying, 'tis no use going, *You were right*—we move at 11 o'clock, P.M. Sharp, tonight: all right, then, there's no sleep for your humble again tonight.

2d night's loss of sleep.

If it took a minute to cross that pack train over the "Muddy", it took two hours; other side of creek Colonel Keogh hunted me up, he being the officer in charge of rear guard;—he was making the very air sulphuruous with blue oaths, telling me of the situation; however, from having been there very many times myself, I knew it better than he did: so I consoled him with, "Never mind old man, do the best you can, and it will all come out right."

I don't begin to believe that Job ever had much to do with shaved tailed pack mules.

Well, my advice seemed to brace Col. Keogh a bit, and I kept the ding-donging of the tin cup, frying pan—or something, that was my guide as to direction, the pounding of that on the saddle of the horse on the left of the troop preceding mine, being all I had to go by, the night being pitch dark, and the gait was a trot, so I hadn't much time to swap words with Col. Keogh, or, my guide would be gone.

This trot was kept up for perhaps eight or ten miles; then, came a halt, no orders for same being received, and no orders for anything received by me. So, the Packs remained on mules; saddles & bridles on horses. I crouched down by a sage bush until daylight, and there spied Colonel Reno and little Benny Hodgson going for coffee, hardtack & Trimmings. I invited myself to assist in disposing of that repast; and met with a "1st Class' welcome at suggesting it.

In a few moments, it seemed, the column moved forward, no orders however, for same were gotten, but my troop & I followed the procession: then came almost as sudden a halt: no orders for that. The rear of column knew of none, however, a few moments brought us a summons thro' an orderly, to "Officers' Call," at Head Quarters: when there, General Custer notified us that he had been on the mountain to the left, where our Scouts (Crows) were all the night; that they had told him thro. the interpreter, that they could see dust, indians and ponies, & all that. He could see nothing through the old telescopic glass they had and didn't believe there was anything to be seen; now, strange perhaps to say, I did believe it:—another "Pre." I knew it, because, why, I'd sooner trust the sharp eye of an indian than to trust a pretty good binocular that I always carried; and I'd gotten that from experience. However, 'twasn't my "chip in," so I said nothing. At this halt General Custer notified us that the first troop commander who notified him that the requirements of an order issued a few days before were being carried out strictly in the troop, that officer and troop should have the post of honor, the advance. I notified him at once that in my

Indian country, 1876. Calamity Peak, South Dakota.

119

Sketch of Benteen by the author.

-MICK ANGLO-

Custer's Last Stand, film
version. Robert Shaw, as
Custer, prepares for the finale.

Sketch of General Custer by the author.

– MICK ANGLO –

General Custer and his
scouts, 1874. Bloody Knife
kneeling by Custer's shoulder.

troop the requirements were being strictly adhered to. I feel quite sure it wasn't expected from me; but he stammered out, Well, Col. Benteen, Your troop has the advance.

When all had reported, I was ordered to move in advance with my troop, which I did, but had gone but a short distance when General Custer rode up, saying, I was setting the pace too fast. He then rode in advance; and after going a few miles the command was halted between hills on every side, and Genl. Custer and his adjutant stepped aside, and were figuring on paper for quite awhile, atwhat, we knew not. However, when thro, I was called up and notified that my command was 3 Troops, and that I would move to the left to a line of bluffs about 2 miles away. Sending out an officer and a few men as advance guard, to "pitch in" to anything I came across, and to notify him at once; I started on my mission immediately:—this was just about 15 miles from where I found the dead body of Genl. Custer 3 days afterwards.

I omitted stating, that while en route obeying Custer's last order, I received two other orders from him, and these through the Chief Trumpeter and the Sergeant Major of the regiment; the first to the effect, that, should I not find anything at the first line of bluffs, then, to go on to the second line of bluffs, to pitch in, and notify him at once, being included: the order through Sergt. Major received 15 or 20 minutes later, was, if nothing could be seen from second line of bluffs, then, to go on until I came to a valley, to "pitch in," and to notify him at once, being also included: now, all of this time the balance of the regiment was on the march, and the last glimpse I had of them was the grayhorse troop in rapid motion. I thought of course they had struck something. However, I had that valley to find, and away we went for it, myself and orderly being in advance of the advance guard. The 2d line of bluffs showed no valley,—only bluffs & bluffs:—so, another of my "Prees." came; and said, old man, that crowd ahead is going to strike a snag: indians have too much sense to travel over such country as you have been going unless they are terribly pushed; so, you'd better get back to that trail, and you will find work; then "Right Oblique" was the word until we got out of the hills to the trail; my command getting to it just ahead of the train of Packs, the horses not having been watered since evening before, and this being along about one o'clock P. M. of a hot June day, they were needing it badly. So, on the trail I halted at a morass for a few moments for the purpose of giving the men and animals a chance at it. I attended to the watering of the horse I was riding, for the brute was tricky, and unless you took the precaution to lariat him to something, after the bit was taken from his mouth, and he thro' drinking, you could not hold him by the strap of halter: no one could: and away he would go; and when he got good and ready, he would rejoin the troop. Well, at this watering, I lariated old Dick to a stump of iron wood before removing the bit; and after drinking he pulled up taut on the stump, and looked as if to say, "Well, I didn't much care to go off this time anyway": but that was the time of times, old fellow, for you would have been saved two wounds, and two days where water was worth its weight in green backs, though beautiful and blue, within a stone's throw from our stand.

121

I dismounted, after riding around the lodge, peeped in, and saw the body of an indian on a scaffold or cot of rude poles. By this time the battalion was up— and away we went again. A mile or two brought orders through a Sergeant to the officer in charge of pack-train. I told him where I had last seen it— another couple of miles brought an order for me thro' the orderly trumpeter of day, from the adjutant of regiment, to the effect:

Benteen, Big Village, Be quick; Bring Packs.

P.S. Bring Packs,

W. W. Cooke,

Adjt.

Well, the Packs were safe behind. I knew *that—better than anybody*. I couldn't waste time in going back, nor in halting where I was for them. So, we went— V.V.V.

I resume with the last order received from the Adjutant of the 7th Cavalry; the last lines penciled by him, viz: "Benteen, Come on, Big Village, Be Quick, Bring Packs. P. S. Bring Packs. John Martini, the trumpeter, bringing this dispatch was a thick headed, dull witted Italian, just about as much cut out for a cavalryman as he was for a King: he informed me that the indians were "skedaddling"; hence, less the necessity for retracing our steps to get the Packs, and the same would be gained by awaiting the arrival of them where we then were. We did neither; but took the Trot! and, from the ford where Reno first crossed the beautifully blue Little Big Horn we saw going on what evidently was not "skedaddling" on the part of the indians, as there were 12 or 14 dis- mounted men on the river bottom, and they were being ridden down and shot by 800 or 900 indian warriors.

We concluded that the lay of the land had better be investigated a bit, as so much of the Italian trumpeter's story hadn't "Panned out." So—off to left I went, seeing a group of 3 or 4 Absaraka or Crow Indians; from them I learned this; Otoe Sioux, Otoe Sioux, the "Otoe" meaning innumerable, or —Heaps of them—and we soon found that there were enough of them.

From the point I saw the Crows. I got the first sight of the men of Reno's battalion who had retreated from the river bottom, recrossed the river a couple of miles below, and were showing up on the bluffs on the side of the river that my battalion had kept and was then on: the battalion being in line. Reno, knowing of course we were soldiers, came riding to meet me as I moved towards him. My first query of Reno was—where is Custer? Showing him the last order received from the Adjutant of Regt., Reno replied that he did not know, that Custer had ordered him across the river to charge the indians, informing him that he would support him with the whole "Outfit," but he had neither seen nor heard from him since:—Well, our battalion got just in the nick of time to save Reno's.

After a few words with Col. Reno I inquired as to the whereabouts of "D"

Troop of my Battn.—and was informed that Capt. Weir had, without orders, gone down the river. This being the case, I sallied after Weir, and about $\frac{3}{4}$ths of a mile lower down, from the top of the highest point in vicinity, saw Weir's troop returning; hordes of indians hurrying them somewhat. Reno came to same point after I had thrown Captain French's troop in line at right angle with river, to hold that point, dismounted, till Weir's troop got thro, and to then retreat slowly, and I would have that part of command looked after. This didn't finish as well as I had hoped and expected it would. However, from fact of the indians not making the most of the opportunity, and Lieut. Ed. S. Godfrey carrying out his instructions more faithfully and in a more soldierly manner, we had time sufficient to get some kind of a line formed: the first officer I saw when establishing a line, was Lieutenant Geo. D. Wallace, recently killed by some of the same Sioux, at the "Wounded Knee" fight in Dak. I said, Wallace, put the right of your troop here. His answer was, "I have no troop, only three men." Well, said I, stay here with your three men, and don't let them get away, I will have you looked out for:—and Wallace and the three men stayed, and they were looked out for. Col. Reno was on the left—forming the same line—which wasn't a line but an arc of a circle, rather irregularly described too. And when we met about centre, my own Troop remained to be disposed of, so I put it over much ground, almost as much as the other six companies occupied, protecting left flank, and well to the rear, just on the edge of line of bluffs, near river.

The formation as described, was dismounted; the horses of command, being placed in a saucer like depression of prairie, the lower rim of the saucer, instead of a rim was a gentle slope. The hospital was established at the upper rim, and was about as safe a place as there was around the vicinity, the blue canopy of heaven being the covering: the sage brushes, sand being the operating board: but the stout heart and nervy skilful hand of Dr. Porter (the only surgeon of the three of command that hadn't been killed), was equal to the occasion.

I state but the facts when I say that we had a fairly warm time with those red men as long as sufficient light was left for them to draw a bead on us, and the same I'm free to maintain, in the language of Harte.

I don't know how many of the miscreants there were—probably we shall never know—but there were enough.

Now, be it remembered, this wasn't a fight instituted by the army for glory going purposes, or anything of that kind; but rather, was a little gentle disciplining which the Department of the Interior (the Department of U. S. Government having charge of the Indian Bureau), had promised would be given the indians if they, the nomads of the tribe, declined to come in to agencies in the Spring; be good, and draw their pay; runners having been sent out to the self supporters; i.e. those, who gave the Agencies the grand go by, as it were, to the effect, that if they didn't report, Soldiers would be sent out to bring them in. About the only answer that they returned as far as I wot, was "We will be here when you come for us"! and sure enough, they were there! but little thought anyone that they would be in such hordes.

Private J. W. Gardiner of the
Ninth Cavalry.

I judged of the condition of the men of my troop somewhat by my own condition; though that is one of almost physical never tire; but not having had sleep for the two nights previous to this one, was getting just a trifle weary myself; so, up and down the line of "H" Troop 1st Lieut. Gibson and myself tramped, the night of June 25th & 26th, doing our very best to keep the sentinels awake, but we just could not do it. Kicking them; well, they didn't care anything about that. However, we two kept awake on our end of line, and at early daybreak ascertained that few, if any of our red friends had given up hope of doing us up. The clatter they made stirred our little bivouac out pretty effectually, then *all* being on the qui vive; thinking the situation was O.K. that I'd try and "Round Up" a few lines of sleep, to make up somewhat for the three night's sleep that I was short of. So, down I dropped on the hill-side, determined to gather what I could, in; but some wakeful red skin had pretty nearly my exact range, plumping me in the heel of extended boot; another bullet scattered the dry dust under my arm pit; however, I hadn't the remotest idea of letting little things like that disturb me, and think that I at least had gotten forty winks, when a Sergeant of my troop informed me that Lieut. Gibson of my troop was having a regular monkey & parrot time of it: to say that I felt like saying something naughty to that Sergeant, was putting it mildly, but down I ran and thro and thro' the pack train, getting together some 15 or 16 soldiers & packers, making them carry up sacks of bacon, boxes of hard bread, pack-saddles, and materials of that kind;— quite a sufficiency to build a respectable little breast work— which, after propping up as well as we could, I turned over with the Falstaffian crowd, to "Gib." my 1st lieutenant, telling him to hold the fort, notwithstanding what might become of us. Then I walked along the front of my troop and told them that I was getting mad, and I wanted them to charge down the ravines with me when I gave the yell: then, each to yell as if provided with a thousand throats. The Chinese act was sufficiently good enough for me if it would work; but I hadn't so much real trust in its efficacy. However, when the throttles of the "H sters" were given full play, and we dashed into the unsuspecting savages who were amusing themselves by throwing clods of dirt, arrows by hand, and otherwise, for simply pure cussedness among us, to say that 'twas a surprise to them, is mild form, for they somersaulted and vaulted as so many trained acrobats, having no order in getting down those ravines, but quickly getting; de'il take the hindmost!

Then, then, I had the key to the beautiful blue water that had been flowing so ripplingly at our very feet for two days—and which wounded and well longed so much for,—there it was, ours, for the getting. Well, 'twasn't the simplest of matters to get a camp-kettle of it, even then, but as we were on the brink of it, to none did it occur to picture or think of how it had to be gotten; we proceeded to get it, but at the expense of many wounded, and this for the sake of the already wounded as well as the dry as dust living. Speaking for myself, I am quite sure that I would gladly and cheerfully have given the very prettiest and newest twenty dollar silver certificate that I might have persuaded my first lieutenant to have lent me, for just one Oz. of Spiritus Frumenti to have dashed into just about same quantity of that pure Little Big Horn water, if for no other purpose

128

than to just brace me a bit, for to a certainty I was "Plumb" tired out and sleepy too. However, the business for the day had only fairly opened: and I got no chance to steal off and sleep, or bless me if I would not have done it.

To say that I ever had more serene satisfaction at killing a Black tailed buck deer, on the bound, with a carbine, than I had in putting one of Uncle Sam's 45s thro' as noble a specimen of the Dakotas as ever fluttered an eagle feather in his scalp lock, was every word true at that time; though I'm rather fond of indians than otherwise, but to plump him thro' his spinal, as he was cavorting thro the ravines, there being so many of them around, that one wouldn't be missed, and being so confoundedly mad and sleepy, must say that I looked on that dead red with exquisite satisfaction and not because he was maiden hair either, for he wasn't—but I was so tired, and they wouldn't let me sleep. Now, Strong man, I, a bit out of luck in losing the 1st night's sleep in the category of three, still, how tired must my good friend Dr. Lord have been, when he galloped in with Custer before getting his quietus, and *he* A.H.L., was of weak physique.

SERGEANT MARTIN'S ACCOUNT

A little before 8 o'clock, on the morning of June 25, my captain, Benteen, called me and ordered me to report to General Custer as orderly trumpeter. The regiment was then several miles from the Divide between the Rosebud and the Little Big Horn. We had halted there to make coffee after a night march.

We knew, of course, that plenty of Indians were somewhere near, because we had been going through deserted villages for two days and following a heavy trail from the Rosebud, and on the 24th we had found carcasses of dead buffalo that had been killed and skinned only a short time before.

I reported to the General personally, and he just looked at me and nodded. He was talking to an Indian scout, called Bloody Knife, when I reported, and Bloody Knife was telling him about a big village in the valley, several hundred tepees and about five thousand Sioux. I sat down a little way off and heard the talk. I couldn't understand what the Indian said, but from what the General said in asking questions and his conversation with the interpreter I understood what it was about.

The General was dressed that morning in a blue-gray flannel shirt, buckskin trousers, and long boots. He wore a regular company hat. His yellow hair was cut short—not very short; but it was not long and curly on his shoulders like it used to be.

General Custer. Photo taken at the time of his expedition with Grand Duke Alexis of Russia.

Very soon the General jumped on his horse and rode bareback around the camp, talking to the officers in low tones and telling them what he wanted them to do. By 8.30 the command was ready to march and the scouts went on ahead.

129

We followed slowly, about fifteen minutes later. I rode about two yards back of the General. We moved on, at a walk, until about two hours later we came to a deep ravine, where we halted. The General left us there and went away with the scouts. I didn't go with him, but stayed with the Adjutant. This was when he went up to the "Crow's-nest" on the Divide, to look for the Sioux village that Bloody Knife had told him about. He was gone a long time, and when he came back they told him about finding fresh pony tracks close by, and that the Sioux had discovered us in the ravine. At once he ordered me to sound officers' call, and I did so. This showed that he realized now that we could not surprise the Sioux, and so there was no use to keep quiet any longer. For two days before this there had been no trumpet calls, and every precaution had been taken to conceal our march. But now all was changed.

The officers came quickly, and they had an earnest conference with the General. None of the men were allowed to come near them, but soon they separated and went back to their companies.

Then we moved on again, and after a while, about noon, crossed the Divide. Pretty soon the General said something to the Adjutant that I could not hear, and pointed off to the left. In a few minutes Captain Benteen, with three troops, left the column and rode off in the direction that the General had been pointing. I wondered where they were going, because my troop was one of them.

The rest of the regiment rode on, in two columns—Colonel Reno, with three troops, on the left, and the other five troops, under General Custer, on the right. I was riding right behind the General. We followed the course of a little stream that led in the direction of the Little Big Horn River. Reno was on the left bank and we on the right.

All the time, as we rode, scouts were riding in and out, and the General would listen to them and sometimes gallop away a short distance to look around. Sometimes Reno's column was several hundred yards away and sometimes it was close to us, and then the General motioned with his hat and they crossed over to where we were.

Soon we came to an old tepee that had a dead warrior in it. It was burning. The Indian scouts had set it afire. Just a little off from that there was a little hill, from which Girard, one of the scouts, saw some Indians between us and the river. He called to the General and pointed them out. He said they were running away. The General ordered the Indian scouts to follow them, but they refused to go. Then the General motioned to Colonel Reno, and when he rode up the General told the Adjutant to order him to go down and cross the river and attack the Indian village, and that he would support him with the whole regiment. He said he would go down to the other end and drive them, and that he would have Benteen hurry up and attack them in the center.

Reno, with his three troops, left at once, on a trot, going toward the river, and we followed for a few hundred yards, and then swung to the right, down the river.

The buffalo hunters.

We went at a gallop, too. (Just stopped once to water the horses). The General seemed to be in a big hurry. After we had gone about a mile or two we came to a big hill that overlooked the valley, and we rode around the base of it and halted. Then the General took me with him, and we rode to the top of the hill, where we could see the village in the valley on the other side of the river. It was a big village, but we couldn't see it all from there, though we didn't know it then; but several hundred tepees were in plain sight.

There were no bucks to be seen; all we could see was some squaws and children playing and a few dogs and ponies. The General seemed both surprised and glad, and said the Indians must be in their tents, asleep.

We did not see anything of Reno's column when we were up on the hill. I am sure the General did not see them at all, because he looked all around with his glasses, and all he said was that we had "got them this time."

He turned in the saddle and took off his hat and waved it so the men of the command, who were halted at the base of the hill, could see him, and he shouted to them, "Hurrah, boys, we've got them! We'll finish them up and then go home to our station."

Then the General and I rode back down to where the troops were, and he talked a minute with the Adjutant, telling him what he had seen. We rode on, pretty fast, until we came to a big ravine that led in the direction of the river, and the General pointed down there and then called me. This was about a mile down the river from where we went up on the hill, and we had been going at a trot and gallop all the way. It must have been about three miles from where we left Reno's trail.

The General said to me, "Orderly, I want you to take a message to Colonel Benteen. Ride as fast as you can and tell him to hurry. Tell him it's a big village and I want him to be quick, and to bring the ammunition packs." He didn't stop at all when he was telling me this, and I just said, "Yes, sir," and checked my horse, when the Adjutant said, "Wait, orderly, I'll give you a message," and he stopped and wrote it in a big hurry, in a little book, and then tore out the leaf and gave it to me.

And then he told me, "Now, orderly, ride as fast as you can to Colonel Benteen. Take the same trail we came down. If you have time, and there is no danger, come back; but otherwise stay with your company."

My horse was pretty tired, but I started back as fast as I could go. The last I saw of the command they were going down into the ravine. The gray horse troop was in the center and they were galloping.

The Adjutant had told me to follow our trail back, and so in a few minutes I was back on the same hill again where the General and I had looked at the village; but before I got there I heard firing back of me, and I looked around and saw Indians, some waving buffalo robes and some shooting. They had been in ambush.

Drawing of a cavalryman by Winslow Homer (1836-1910). Published in *Harper's Weekly*.

133

Bismark, Dakota, 1876.
Bismark was the nearest
town to Fort Abraham
Lincoln.

The *Custer Route* to
Bismark from Deadwood,
served the Black Hills area.

134

Just before I got to the hill I met Boston Custer. He was riding at a run, but when he saw me he checked his horse and shouted "Where's the General?" and I answered, pointing back of me, "Right behind that next ridge you'll find him." And he dashed on. That was the last time he was ever seen alive.

When I got up on the hill, I looked down and there I saw Reno's battalion in action. It had been not more than ten or fifteen minutes since the General and I were on the hill, and then we had seen no Indians. But now there were lots of them, riding around and shooting at Reno's men, who were dismounted and in skirmish line. I don't know how many Indians there were—a lot of them. I did not have time to stop and watch the fight; I had to get on to Colonel Benteen; but the last I saw of Reno's men they were fighting in the valley and the line was falling back.

Some Indians saw me, because right away they commenced shooting at me. Several shots were fired at me—four or five, I think—but I was lucky and did not get hit. My horse was struck in the hip, though I did not know it until later.

It was a very warm day and my horse was hot, and I kept on as fast as I could go. I didn't know where Colonel Benteen was, nor where to look for him, but I knew I had to find him.

I followed our trail back to the place we had watered our horses, and looked all round for Colonel Benteen. Pretty soon I saw his command coming. I was riding at a jog trot then. My horse was all in and I was looking everywhere for Colonel Benteen.

As soon as I saw them coming I waved my hat to them and spurred my horse, but he couldn't go any faster. But it was only a few hundred yards before I met Colonel Benteen. He was riding quite a distance in front of the troops, with his orderly trumpeter, at a fast trot. The nearest officer to him was Captain Weir, who was at the head of his troop, about two or three hundred yards back.

I saluted and handed the message to Colonel Benteen, and then I told him what the General said—that it was a big village and to hurry. He said, "Where's the General now?" and I answered that the Indians we saw were running, and I supposed that by this time he had charged through the village. I was going to tell him about Major Reno being in action, too, but he didn't give me the chance. He said, "What's the matter with your horse?" and I said, "He's just tired out, I guess." The Colonel said, "Tired out? Look at his hip," and then I saw the blood from the wound. Colonel Benteen said, "You're lucky it was the horse and not you." By this time Captain Weir had come up to us, and Colonel Benteen handed the message to him to read and told me to join my company.

He didn't give me any order to Captain McDougall, who was in command of the rear guard, or to Lieutenant Mathey, who had the packs. I told them so at Chicago in 1879, when they had the court of inquiry, but I didn't speak English so good then, and they misunderstood me and made the report of my testimony show that I took an order to Captain McDougall. But this is a mistake.

Captain Jack, the poet scout
who recited maudlin poems
on the stage. On his left is
an actor.

They gave me another horse and I joined my troop and rode on with them. The pack-train was not very far behind then. It was in sight, maybe a mile away, and the mules were coming along, some of them walking, some trotting, and others running. We moved on faster than the packs could go, and soon they were out of sight, except that we could see their dust.

We followed General Custer's trail until we got near the ridge where the General and I had first seen the village. We could see the fight going on in the valley, and Reno's command was retreating to the side of the river we were on. As we approached them, Colonel Reno came out to meet us. He was dismounted, his hat was gone, and he had a handkerchief tied around his forehead. He was out of breath and excited, and raised his hand and called to Colonel Benteen. We all heard him. He said, "For God's sake, Benteen, halt your command and help me. I've lost half my men." Part of his men were still coming up the hill, some mounted and some dismounted, and the Indians were firing at them from the hills and ravines near by. They were pretty much excited and disorganized when we got there.

Colonel Benteen said, "Where's Custer?" and Colonel Reno answered, "I don't know. He went off downstream and I haven't seen or heard anything of him since."

We heard a lot of firing down the river; it kept up for a half hour or maybe more. It sounded like a big fight was going on, and the men thought it was General Custer, and that he was whipping the Indians, and we all wanted to hurry on and join him, but they wouldn't let us go. Captain Weir had some words with Colonel Reno, and I could tell by the way he was acting that he was excited and angry. He waved his arms and gestured and pointed down the river. Then we heard some volleys, and Captain Weir jumped on his horse and started down the river all alone. But his troop followed him right away.

The rest of us stayed there until the packs all arrived. The ammunition mules came first, in about fifteen minutes; but it was more than an hour before the last pack-mule was up.

Then we started down the river; but by the time we got as far as where Captain Weir had gone with his company, we had to stop, because the Indians had seen us and were coming up the river toward us by the thousand. The firing down below had all stopped by that time, except for an occasional shot, and we thought that they had stood off the General and that he had gone to join General Terry. We did not suspect then that he and all his men had been killed.

We got down about a mile, or maybe a little more, from the hill where we had found Colonel Reno, and then the Indians came on so thick and fast we had to fall back to the hill again.

By that time they were all around us, and more coming all the time, and we had a hot fight until it was dark.

The next morning it started again before day-light, and they kept it up until

The Indian tamed. A
reservation Indian at the turn
of the century.

the middle of the afternoon. They killed a great many of our horses and mules, and a lot of men were killed and wounded, but we stood them off.

I was in America only two years then, and this was my first Indian fight. I had been in the Black Hills with General Custer in 1875, and we had seen plenty of Indians there, but did not fight them.

I admired General Custer very much; all the men did. He was a fighter and not afraid of anything. But he tried to do more than he could that day. They were too many for us, and good fighters, too. They had better weapons than we had and they knew the ground. It is lucky that any of us escaped alive. I don't think we would but for the fact that they heard that General Terry was coming.

I am an old man now and have served the United States a long time since I came from Italy in 1873. I enlisted in 1874 and was in the army for thirty years. My memory isn't as good as it used to be, but I can never forget the battle of the Little Big Horn and General Custer.

I have two sons in the army, and one of them is named for the General. I want them both to be as good soldiers as their father was.

It's a long time since I rode with Custer to his last fight—forty-six years—but I still have the old trumpet that I blew officers' call with the morning of that fatal day, and still have a lively recollection of, as I have a deep affection for, my old General.

JOHN MARTIN
Sergeant, U. S. Army, retired.

LETTER FROM PRIVATE MORRIS

September 21, 1904

I have read your article entitled "War with the Sioux," and as a survivor of Reno's Battalion desire to enter an earnest protest against the many incorrect statements of alleged facts. Col. Reno was cruelly libeled while he was alive, and took his medicine manfully, knowing that he had the respect of every officer and enlisted man who served under him on the 25th and 26th days of June, 1876.

The 7th Cavalry had no use for cowards, and had Reno showed the white feather, he would have been damned by every member of his command. As a matter of fact, we revere his memory as that of a brave and gallant officer, who, through circumstances over which he had no control, was blamed by the public, who had no personal knowledge of the facts for the result of the Battle of the Little Horn. It is quite evident to me that you have never interviewed a single member of Reno's Battalion, to wit: Troops "A," "G," and "M," for if you had you would not misstate the facts, as I assume that you intend to be fair and would not intentionally mislead the public mind.

139

I was a member of Capt. Thomas H. French's Troop "M," 7th U. S. Cavalry, and I submit the following as a concise statement of the facts: We lost sight of Custer, whose command was on our right, at least thirty minutes before we crossed the Little Horn River. We saw a party of about one hundred Indians before we reached the river; we pursued them across the Little Horn and down the valley. As soon as we forded, Reno gave the command, "Left into line, gallop—forward, guide, center," and away we went faster than I had ever ridden before. The Indians rode as fast as they could, and the battalion in line of battle after them. A body of at least two thousand came up the valley to meet the one hundred or more we were pursuing. They immediately made a flank movement to our left and a stand, opened a galling fire, causing some of our horses to become unmanageable. John R. Meyer's horse carried him down the valley through the Indians, some of whom chased him two or three miles over the hills and back to ford. He escaped with a gun-shot wound in the neck. Rutten's horse also ran away, but he succeeded in making a circle before reaching the Indians, and received only a gun-shot wound in the shoulder. We were then abreast the timber; to continue the charge down the valley meant (to the mind of every one) immediate destruction of the battalion, which consisted of about one hundred and twenty men (the old guard, of ten men from each troop, being with the packs).

Reno, very properly, gave the command "Battalion halt—prepare to fight on foot—dismount!" He directed French to send ten men from the right of his troop to skirmish the woods, before the "numbers four" proceeded there with the horses. We immediately deployed as skirmishers and opened fire. The odds were at least thirty to one, as our line with the fours out did not exceed seven officers and ninety men. We had, however, a few Indian scouts and civilians. We had entire confidence in our officers and in ourselves, and went to work smiling and as cool as if we were at target practice. In less time than it takes to relate it, the Indians were on three sides of us. We were ordered to lie down, and every man that I could see, except Reno and French, were fighting lying down. Reno walked along the line giving instructions to the men, while French was calling his men's attention to his own marksmanship with an infantry long-tom that he carried.

While in this position, the man next on my right, Sergeant O'Hara, was killed. The smoke obscured the line, but bullets were taking effect all along it. We were perfectly cool, determined, and doing good execution and expected to hear Custer attack. We had been fighting lying down about fifteen minutes when one of our men came from the timber and reported that they were killing our horses in the rear. Every troop had, at this time, suffered loss and the enemy was closing in, despite our steady and deadly fire. Reno then made his only error; he gave the command, "Retreat to your horses, men!" French immediately corrected the mistake with the command, "Steady, men—fall back, slowly; face the enemy, and continue your fire." "M" troop fell back slowly and in perfect order, held the Indians in check until "A" and "G" had mounted.

Red Cloud, implacable enemy of the white man, finally submitted to his rule.

Several of their horses had been shot, and their riders, consequently, very much disturbed.

"M" Troop left Sergeant O'Hara and Private Smith on the skirmish line. Isaiah, the colored interpreter of Fort Rice, Bloody Knife, the Chief of the Rees Scouts, and a civilian also remained. Lawrence was hit in the stomach when about to mount. I went to his relief, which caused me to be the last man to leave the timber, with the command, with the exception of Lieutenant Hare, who passed me in the bottom. Sergeant Charles White was wounded in the arm and his horse killed. He was left in the woods, as was also "Big Fritz", a Norwegian, whose surname I do not remember, but whose horse was killed. "A" and "G" had men left in the timber also, and they all reached the command on the hill during the night with De Rudio, or about the same time.

I give more details in regard to "M" than the other troops, because of a personal acquaintance with each member. Corporal Scollen and Private Sommers fell in the charge from the timber to the ford. It was a charge and not a retreat, and it was led by Reno. Every man that I saw used his revolver at close range. I was at least twenty yards behind the rear of the command. The Indians closed in, so I was compelled to jump my horse off the bank, at least fifty yards below the ford, and while in the river had an excellent view of the struggle. It was hand to hand, and McIntosh was certainly there at the ford and sold his life as dearly as he possibly could. When I reached the cut in bank, I found Turley and Rye mounted and Lieutenant Hodgson wounded and dismounted. He was waist-deep in the water. He grasped my off stirrup strap with both hands. Rye let Turley go ahead through the cut, and he was killed as he reached the top; Rye followed without receiving a scratch. The lieutenant held onto my stirrup for two or three seconds, and was dragged out of the water. He was hit again, and let go as my horse plunged up the cut. Sergeant Criswell may have assisted him out of the water, but if he did he went back into it again. To say that any man could or did ride back down that cut is to suggest, to my mind, the impossible. Upon reaching the level above the cut I dismounted and led my horse as fast as possible up the bluff, and overtook Tinker, Bill Meyer and Gordon about half way up the bluff. We stopped a moment to rest. The bodies of the fallen soldiers were plainly visible. They marked the skirmish line and the line of the charge from the timber to the ford, and were in the river and at the top of the cut. At this instant a shower of lead sent Meyer and Gordon to the happy hunting-ground, and a fifty caliber passed through the left breast of your humble servant. Our horses were also hit. I continued up the hill alone and joined the command; was then assisted to the improvised hospital.

Reno at this time had lost, in killed, wounded, and left dismounted in the woods, over 30 per cent. of his battalion (there were over ten left in the woods). Lieutenant Hare was particularly conspicuous, and distinguished himself by his cool and determined manner when he ordered the men to fall in at the top of the hill, and whatever demoralization there was, was immediately dispelled by that courageous young Texan. Benteen, arriving about an hour later, came up as slow as though he were going to a funeral. By this statement I do not desire to reflect in any way upon him; he was simply in no hurry; and Müller, of his troop, who occupied an adjoining cot to mine in the hospital at Fort Abraham Lincoln, told me that they walked all the way, and that they heard the heavy firing while they were watering their horses.

Benteen was, unquestionably, the bravest man I ever met. He held the Indians in absolute contempt, and was a walking target from the time he became engaged until the end of the fight at sundown on the 26th. He took absolute charge of one side of the hill, and you may rest assured that he did not bother Reno for permission of any kind. He was in supreme command of that side of the hill, and seemed to enjoy walking along the line where the bullets were the thickest. His troop, "H" did not dig rifle-pits during the night of the 25th, as the other troops did, and in the morning their casualties were increased on that account. He ordered "M" out of their pits to reinforce his troop. There was some dissatisfaction at the order, as the men believed that the necessity was due solely to the neglect of "H", in digging pits. They obeyed, however, and assisted Benteen in his famous charge.

It was rumored, subsequently, that French recommended his First Sergeant, John Ryan, a sharpshooter, and some other men for medals, and that Benteen refused to indorse the recommendation as to Ryan, because he failed immediately to order the men out of their pits at his end of the line at his (Benteen's) order. It was claimed that French thereupon withdrew his list. Ryan was in charge of the ten men that Reno sent to skirmish the woods.

I was very much amused to learn, from your article, that Windolph received a medal. I remember him as the tailor of "H" troop, and have a distinct recollection of his coming into the field-hospital, bent almost double and asking for treatment for a wound which, his appearance would suggest, was a mortal one, but which the surgeon found, on removing his trousers, to be only a burn. The surgeon ordered him back to the line amid a shout of laughter from the wounded men. Mike Madden of "K" lost his leg, and Tanner of "M" his life, in the dash for the water for the wounded. I hope Madden received a medal.

In view of the conflict between the foregoing and the statements contained in your article, I ask you to investigate the matter further, with a view to correcting the false impression that your readers must have concerning Reno and his command. In conclusion, I ask you "how, in God's name," you could expect Reno, with one hundred and twenty men, to ride through upwards of three thousand armed Sioux, and then be of assistance to Custer or any one else? I say we were sent into that valley and caught in an ambush like rats in a trap. That if we had remained ten minutes longer, there would not have been one left to tell the tale. That the much abused Reno did charge out of the timber, and that we who survive owe our lives to that identical charge which he led. We, at least, give him credit for saving what he did of his command.

WM. E. MORRIS

Late private, Troop "M," Seventh U. S. Cavalry

143

Epitaph. Monument to the
men who died at the
Little Big Horn.

144